the Elephant Whisperer

MY LIFE WITH THE HERD IN THE AFRICAN WILD

LAWRENCE ANTHONY

WITH GRAHAM SPENCE

ADAPTED FOR YOUNG READERS BY THEA FELDMAN

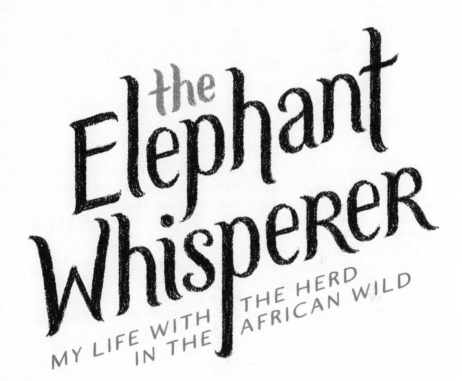

the Elephant Whisperer

MY LIFE WITH THE HERD IN THE AFRICAN WILD

HENRY HOLT AND COMPANY

NEW YORK

Henry Holt and Company, *Publishers since 1866*
Henry Holt® is a registered trademark of Macmillan Publishing Group, LLC.
175 Fifth Avenue, New York, NY 10010
mackids.com

Library of Congress Cataloging-in-Publication Data

Names: Anthony, Lawrence, author. | Spence, Graham, author. | Feldman, Thea, author.
Title: The elephant whisperer (young readers adaptation) : my life with the heard in the
    African wild / Lawrence Anthony with Graham Spence ; adapted by Thea Feldman.
Description: First young readers edition. | New York : Henry Holt and Company, 2017. |
    First edition : 2009. | Audience: Ages 10–14.
Identifiers: LCCN 2017029230 (print) | LCCN 2016058476 (ebook) |
    ISBN 9781627793100 (Ebook) | ISBN 9781627793094 (hardcover)
Subjects: LCSH: African elephant—Conservation—South Africa—Zululand—Juvenile
    literature. | Wildlife refuges—South Africa—Zululand—Juvenile literature. | Anthony,
    Lawrence—Homes and haunts. | Wildlife conservationists—South Africa—Zululand.
Classification: LCC QL737.P98 (print) | LCC QL737.P98 A58 2017 (ebook) |
    DDC 599.67/4—dc23
LC record available at https://lccn.loc.gov/2017029230

Our books may be purchased in bulk for promotional, educational, or business use. Please contact your local bookseller or the Macmillan Corporate and Premium Sales Department at (800) 221-7945 ext. 5442 or by e-mail at MacmillanSpecialMarkets@macmillan.com.

First edition, 2009
First Young Readers edition, 2017
Printed in the United States of America by LSC Communications, Harrisonburg, Virginia

10 9 8 7 6 5 4 3 2 1

To my beautiful, caring Françoise,
for allowing me to be who I am.

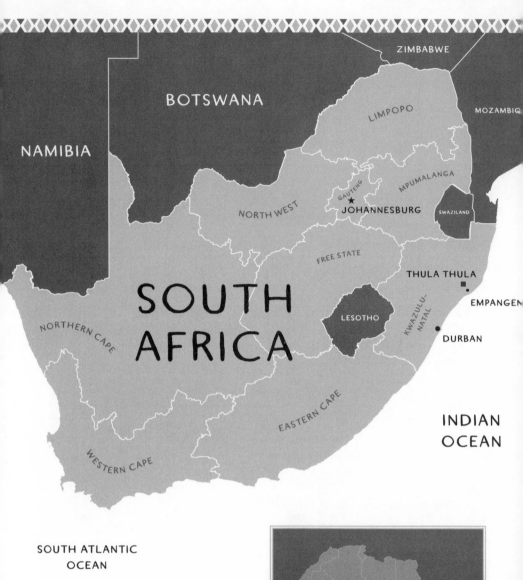

ZIMBABWE

BOTSWANA

NAMIBIA

MOZAMBIQ

LIMPOPO

MPUMALANGA

NORTH WEST

GAUTENG
★
JOHANNESBURG

SWAZILAND

FREE STATE

THULA THULA

EMPANGEN

LESOTHO

KWAZULU-
NATAL

DURBAN

NORTHERN CAPE

SOUTH
AFRICA

EASTERN CAPE

INDIAN
OCEAN

WESTERN CAPE

SOUTH ATLANTIC
OCEAN

N

W   E

S

AFRICA

SOUTH
AFRICA

GLOSSARY

BOMA — a traditional holding pen or enclosure, or a stockade

EMOA — Elephant Managers and Owners Association

KWAZULU-NATAL — the province in South Africa where Thula Thula is located

OVAMBO — an ethnic group in South Africa; the largest ethnic group of Namibia

SPOOR — tracks, usually of an animal, or any sign or trace to follow

ZULU TERMS

AMAGWERAGWER — foreigners

BABBAS — a slang term for babies; Lawrence Anthony's term of endearment for his elephants

HAMBA GAHLE — go well

HAU — an exclamation of surprise

ILANGA — the sun

INDUNA (PLURAL: IZINDUNA) — headman or foreman of a workforce or group

INKHOSI (PLURAL: AMAKHOSI) — overall chief of an ethnic group or clan

MBOMVU — emergency call, equivalent to "Mayday!" or Code Red

MKHULU — grandfather; nickname for Lawrence Anthony by his staff

MNUMZANE — sir

MVULA — rain

NKOSI — title of top-ranking chief

SALE GAHLE — stay well

SAWUBONA — a greeting, literally "I see you"

YEBO — yes

PROLOGUE

In 1999, I was asked to accept a herd of troubled wild elephants on my game reserve, Thula Thula. I had no idea how challenging it would be or how much my life would be enriched.

The adventure has been both physical and spiritual: Physical in the sense that it was action from the word *go*. Spiritual because these giants took me deep into their world.

To be clear, the title of this book is not about me. I make no claim to having any special abilities. Rather, it is about the elephants—they whispered to me and taught me how to listen.

When I describe how the elephants reacted to me, or I to them, it is personal. It is the truth of my own experiences, not the results of planned experiments. I am a conservationist, working to protect wild animals and natural environments. It was through trial and error that I found out what worked best for me and my herd.

Not only am I a conservationist, I am an extremely lucky one. Thula Thula is five thousand acres of undeveloped bush in the heart of Zululand, South Africa. It is the natural home to many local wildlife. This includes the majestic white rhino,

Cape buffalo, leopard, hyena, giraffe, zebra, wildebeest, crocodile, lynx, serval, and many species of antelope. We have seen pythons as long as trucks, and we have possibly the largest breeding population of white-backed vultures in the area.

And, of course, now we have elephants. My elephants were the first wild ones to be reintroduced into our area in more than a century.

I cannot imagine life without them. I don't want a life without them. To understand how they taught me so much, you have to know that communication in the animal kingdom is as natural as a breeze. It was only my own human limitations that got in my way of understanding them at first.

In our noisy cities we tend to forget the things our ancestors knew on a gut level: that the whispers of the wilderness are there for all to hear—and to respond to.

We also have to understand that there are things we *cannot* understand. Elephants possess qualities and abilities well beyond the means of science to decode. Elephants cannot use computers, but they do have superior communication abilities.

My herd showed me that compassion and generosity of spirit is alive and well in the pachyderm kingdom. They showed me that elephants are emotional, caring, and extremely intelligent. They showed me, too, that they value good relationships with humans.

These elephants taught me that all life-forms are important to one another in our common quests for survival and happiness. That there is more to life than just yourself, your own family, or your own kind.

1

Crack! I heard a rifle go off in the distance.

I jumped out of my chair. Then came a burst . . . *crack-crack-crack*. Flocks of squawking birds flew off.

Poachers. On the western boundary.

David, my game ranger, was already sprinting for the Land Rover. I grabbed a shotgun and leapt into the driver's seat. Max, my Staffordshire bull terrier, scrambled onto the seat between us.

As I turned the ignition key and floored the accelerator, David grabbed the two-way radio.

"Ndonga!" he bellowed. "Ndonga, are you receiving? Over!"

Ndonga was the head of my Ovambo guards and a good man to have on your side in a gunfight. But only static greeted David's attempts to contact him. So we powered on alone.

Poachers had been our biggest problem ever since my then-fiancée, Françoise, and I had bought Thula Thula. I couldn't work out who they were or where they were coming from. I had spoken with the *izinduna*, the headmen, of the surrounding Zulu groups. They firmly stated that their people were not involved. I believed them. They also claimed our problems were coming from inside the reserve, but I didn't think that could be true. I had found our employees to be extremely loyal.

It was almost twilight. I slowed as we approached the western fence, killed the headlights, and pulled over behind a large anthill. We eased through a cluster of acacia trees, our nerves on edge, trigger fingers tense, watching and listening. As any game ranger in Africa knows, professional poachers will shoot to kill.

The fence was just fifty yards away. Poachers like to have their escape route open. I motioned to David. He would keep watch while I crawled to the fence to cut off the poachers' retreat if a firefight broke out.

The smell of gunshot spiced the evening air. It hung like a veil in the silence. In Africa, the animals in the bush are only quiet after gunshots.

After a few minutes of absolute stillness, I switched on my flashlight and swept its beam up and down the fence. There were no cuts in it, no holes made by a poacher to get in. And there were no tracks or blood trail to indicate that an animal had been killed and dragged off.

There was nothing but an eerie silence.

Just then, we heard more shots. These came from the eastern edge of the reserve. I realized we had been set up.

Someone had shot off a gun outside the western edge of the reserve to get us to come this way. Now the poachers were shooting nyala—beautiful antelopes—on the far side, at least a forty-five-minute drive away.

We jumped back into the Land Rover and sped off, but I knew it was pointless. The poachers would be off the reserve before we even got close.

I now knew, though, that this was a well-organized criminal operation led by someone who followed our every move. The *izinduna* were right. It *had* to be someone from the inside. How else could they have timed everything so perfectly?

It was pitch-dark when we arrived at the eastern edge of the reserve and traced the scene with our flashlights. We could see flattened, bloodstained grass from where two nyala carcasses had been dragged to and through a hole in the fence. The hole had been crudely hacked with bolt cutters. About ten yards outside the fence were the muddy tracks of a vehicle. That vehicle would, by now, be miles away. The animals would be sold to local butchers who would use them for biltong, a dried meat jerky, which is very popular throughout Africa.

The name *Thula Thula* means "peace and tranquility" in Zulu, and when I bought the land, I vowed no animal would be needlessly killed on my watch. At the time, I didn't realize how difficult that vow would be to keep.

2

The next day I received a phone call from Marion Garaï of the Elephant Managers and Owners Association (EMOA), an elephant-welfare organization made up of several elephant owners in South Africa.

Marion wanted to know if I would be interested in adopting a herd of elephants. Before I could answer, she added that except for the costs of capturing and transporting the elephants, I could have them for free. That, she said, was the good news.

You could have knocked me over with a blade of grass. Elephants? A whole herd of the world's largest land mammals? For a moment I thought it was a joke. I mean, how often do you get called out of the blue and asked if you want a herd of tuskers?

But Marion was serious.

I asked, "What's the bad news?"

Apparently the elephants were considered "troublesome." They tended to break out of reserves, and their current owners wanted to get rid of them fast. If we didn't take them, Marion said, they would be put down—shot. All of them.

"How do they break out?" I asked.

"The matriarch has figured out how to break through electric fences. She just twists the wire around her tusks until it snaps. Or she takes the pain and smashes through. It's unbelievable," said Marion. "The owners have had enough and have now asked EMOA to figure something out."

I pictured the female head of the herd, a five-ton beast, dealing with the shock of 8,000 volts of electricity stabbing through her body. That took determination.

"Also, Lawrence, there are babies involved. I've heard you have a way with animals," she continued. "I reckon Thula Thula's right for them. You're right for them. Or maybe they're right for you."

That floored me. If anything, we were exactly *not* right for a herd of elephants. I was only just getting the reserve up and running properly. And, as the previous day had shown, I was having huge problems with highly organized poachers.

I was about to say no when something held me back. I have always loved elephants. Not only are they the largest and noblest land creatures on this planet, but they symbolize all that is majestic about Africa. And here, unexpectedly, I was being offered my own herd and a chance to help. Would I ever get an opportunity like this again?

"Where're they from?" I asked Marion.

"A reserve in Mpumalanga."

Mpumalanga is the northeastern province of South Africa where most of the country's game reserves—including Kruger National Park—are located.

"How many?"

"Nine. Three adult females, three youngsters, of which one is male, an adolescent bull, and two babies. It's a beautiful family. The matriarch has a gorgeous baby daughter. The young bull, her son, is fifteen years old and an absolutely superb specimen."

"They must be a big problem. Nobody just gives away elephants."

"As I said, the matriarch keeps breaking out. Not only does she snap electric wires, she's also learned how to unlatch gates with her tusks, and the owners aren't too keen about jumbos wandering into the guest camps. If you don't take them, they will be shot. Certainly the adults will be."

I went quiet, trying to unravel all this in my head. The opportunity was great, but so was the risk.

What about the poachers? Would the promise of ivory, an expensive and highly prized material made from an elephant's tusks, bring even more of them out of the woods? What about having to electrify my entire reserve to prevent the giant pachyderms from breaking out? What about having to build an enclosure to quarantine them when they first arrived?

Also, were they just escape artists? Or was this a genuine rogue herd, too dangerous and filled with hatred of humans to keep on a game reserve in a populated area?

The details didn't matter. They were a herd in trouble.

"Yes," I said. "I'll take them."

3

I was reeling from the shock of becoming an instant elephant-owner, when I got another one. The current owners wanted the herd off their property within two weeks. Otherwise the deal would be off, and the elephants would be shot. Unfortunately, when an animal as large as an elephant is considered "troublesome," it is almost always shot.

Two weeks? In that time, we had to repair and electrify twenty miles of big game fencing and build a strong quarantine *boma*—a holding pen—from scratch. We had to build a fence around the *boma* and electrify it with enough mega-volts to prevent a ten-thousand-pound animal from breaking out. The electrical force is not supposed to injure the elephants; it's just supposed to warn them off. It was also vital that the *boma*'s fence be identical to the reserve's outer fence. If the elephants learned that bumping into the *boma*'s fence was not much fun, then later, when they had free range of the reserve, they would steer clear of the border fences, too.

There was no way we were going to be able to do all that in just two weeks, but we would certainly give it a try.

I made David my right-hand man on the project. I then

asked the Zulu staff to put the word out among the local community that we needed workers. Over the next two days, hordes of people showed up outside Thula Thula's gates, clamoring for work. Hundreds of thousands of people in rural Africa live close to the edge. I was glad to be able to contribute to the community.

To keep the *amakhosi*, the local chieftains, on our side, I met with them to explain what we were doing.

In record time, we were up and running. Despite the impossible deadline, a fence slowly crept up across the countryside, and I began to breathe easier.

Then we ran into another problem.

4

David sprinted into the office. "Bad news, boss. Workers on the western boundary have put down their tools. They say they're being shot at. Everyone's too scared to work. What do we do?"

"Let's try and find out what's going on," I answered. "In the meantime, we don't have much choice. Pay off those too jittery to work and let's get replacements. We've got to keep moving."

I also gave instructions for a group of security guards to be placed on standby to protect the remaining workers.

The next morning David came running again.

"Man, we've got real problems," he said, catching his breath. "They're shooting again, and one of the workers is down."

I grabbed my old rifle, and the two of us sped to the fence in the Land Rover. Most of the workers were crouching behind trees, while a couple of them tended to another worker who had been hit in the face by heavy shotgun pellets.

After checking that the man's wounds were not life-threatening, we started crisscrossing the bush until we picked up the tracks, or *spoor* as it is called in Africa. It belonged to a single gunman, not a group, as we had initially feared. I sent Bheki and my security *induna*, or foreman, Ngwenya, whose name means "crocodile" in Zulu, to track the gunman. David and I would stay and protect the workers.

Bheki and Ngwenya spotted the gunman and exchanged fire with him, but the shooter disappeared into the thick bush. To their surprise, they knew him. He was a hunter from another Zulu village some miles away.

We drove the injured worker to the hospital and called the police. The guards identified the gunman, and the cops raided his thatched hut, where they seized an old shotgun. He confessed without any hint of shame that he was a professional poacher. Then he blamed us for building an electric fence that would deprive him of his livelihood. He would no longer be able break into Thula Thula so easily. He denied trying to kill anyone, though. Instead, he said he just wanted to scare off the workers and stop the fence from being finished.

His shotgun was a battered, rusty, double-barrel 12-bore, held together with vinyl electrical tape. There was no way this was also the person responsible for our major poaching problem.

So who was?

5

After this incident, construction continued from dawn to dusk, seven days a week. It was backbreaking work, sweaty and dirty, and during the day temperatures soared to 110 degrees. But mile by mile, the electric fence inched northward, then cut east.

Building the *boma* was also grueling, though on a far smaller scale. We measured out 110 square yards of bush and cemented nine-foot-tall, heavy-duty poles into concrete foundations every twelve yards. Then coils of hardened mesh and a trio of cables as thick as a man's thumb were strung tightly between the poles.

No bush fence will hold a determined elephant without electrified or "hot" wires. We ran four hot wires along the poles. Two energizers run off car batteries would generate the "juice."

Touching a hot wire is not fatal, but the shock is excruciating, even to an elephant with an inch-thick hide. I have experienced the massive punch of a wire's electricity firsthand, several times. I have accidentally touched a wire during repairs or hit one while carelessly waving my arms in animated conversation, much to the amusement of my rangers. The electricity seizes and surprises you. Your body shudders, and unless you let go quickly, you sit down involuntarily as your legs collapse. The only good thing is that you recover quickly enough.

Once the fence was up, the final task was to chop down any trees that an elephant could push over and onto the wires. That is an elephant's favorite way to snap the current.

A *boma* fence.

The two-week deadline passed in the blink of an eye and, of course, we were nowhere near finished, despite having had men working around the clock on the *boma*. We even worked by car lights at night.

Soon the telephones started jangling with the Mpumalanga reserve managers wanting to know what was going on.

"Everything's fine," I boomed cheerfully over the phone, lying through my teeth. If they knew the problems we had with unrealistic deadlines and workers being shot at by a rogue gunman, they probably would have called the deal off.

Then one day we got the call I dreaded.

The herd had broken out again, and this time damaged three of the reserve's lodges. We were bluntly told that unless we took the elephants immediately, the owners would have to make a "decision."

Françoise fielded the call. She crossed her fingers and said we only needed to get our elephant proofing approved by KwaZulu-Natal (KZN) Wildlife, the province's official authority.

Somehow the owners believed her and reluctantly agreed to an extension. But just a few more days, they warned, or else there would be a "decision."

That word again.

6

The workers were exhausted and still hammering in fence nails when the Mpumalanga reserve manager phoned to say he could wait no longer and was sending the elephants, ready or not. The pachyderms were being loaded as we spoke and would arrive at Thula Thula within eighteen hours.

I hurriedly called KZN Wildlife to come and inspect the *boma*. Fortunately, they said an inspector would be at Thula Thula within a couple of hours.

David and I sped down for a final look-see. I wanted everything to be perfect. But while we were double-checking that all trees were beyond toppling distance from the fence, I realized that something didn't look right.

Then I saw the problem. The fence, including the heavy-duty cables, had been strung up on the outside of the poles instead of on the inside of the poles. That meant the poles provided flimsy support, at best. If an elephant braved the power and leaned on the mesh, it would rip off the posts like paper. The inspector would see this instantly and not approve the fence. The truck would be turned back, and the herd sent to certain death.

I clenched my fists in exasperation. How could we make such a basic error? And why hadn't I noticed it before? It was too late to do anything about it. The dust mushrooming above the savannah signaled the inspector's arrival. I hoped we could bluff our way through, but inwardly I despaired. The elephant rescue project was doomed before it began.

The inspector was a decent guy and knew his business. He made particular note of a large tambouti tree with gnarled bark that was close to the fence. Tambouti is an exceptionally hard wood, and the inspector remarked that not even an elephant could snap this particularly "muscular" tree. He deemed it safe.

Then he went to check the meshing, and my mouth went dry. Surely he'd notice the wire was on the wrong side. But to my gut-churning relief, he didn't spot the obvious mistake. The *boma* was given the green light. I now had my crucial authorization.

When the inspector left, I summoned every available hand to secure the fence correctly before the elephants arrived. While we were working, I got the news that the herd's matriarch and her baby had been shot during the capture. The justification was that she was "bad news" and would lead breakouts at Thula Thula. I was stunned. This was exactly what we were fighting to prevent.

I understood the reasoning behind the choice to kill the

matriarch. Because elephants are so big and dangerous, if they create problems and pose a risk to lodges and tourists, it is quite common for them to be shot. I felt that decision, however, should have been mine to make.

I was convinced that I would be able to settle the herd in their new home. I had been prepared to take the risk of accepting the escape-artist matriarch and her baby and to work with her. This killing cemented my determination to save the rest of the herd.

7

The Zulus, who live close to the land, have a saying that if it rains on the day of a special occasion, the event will be blessed. For those in step with the natural world, rain is life. The day the elephants arrived, it didn't just rain, it poured. The skies sent down torrents, and I wasn't too sure the Zulus had the "blessed" part right. When the truck carrying the elephants arrived outside Thula Thula in thick darkness, the deluge had turned the dirt tracks into streams of mud.

We had barely opened the gates when a tire burst. The popping rubber sounded as loud as a rifle shot. This panicked the elephants, who had just seen their leader gunned down. They started thumping the inside of the trailer like it was a gigantic drum, while the crews worked feverishly to change the wheel.

As soon as the spare wheel had been bolted on, to the surprise of no one, the truck slid a few yards and sank into the mud. Its tires spun without gaining traction and spewed muck all over the place. Even worse, the elephants inside were becoming more and more agitated.

"We've got to sort this out quickly or we're going to have to release them right here," said Kobus Raadt, the vet who was in charge of the transport. "They cannot stay in the truck any longer. Let's just pray the outer fence holds them."

We both knew that with this hair-trigger herd, it wouldn't. We also both knew that if the elephants escaped, they would be shot.

Fortunately the driver, sick of all the talk, took matters into his own hands. Without a word, he slammed the truck into reverse, and somehow moved the huge rig out of the mud. The truck veered onto the savannah, where there was just a bit more for the tires to grip on to. Dodging tire-shredding thornbush and snaking past huge termite mounds, he somehow kept momentum until he reached the *boma*.

The crew cheered as though he had scored a winning goal at the World Cup.

Coaxing the animals from the truck was the next problem. Because of their massive size, elephants are the only animals that can't jump at all. Knowing this, we had already dug a trench for the truck to reverse into so the trailer's floor would be level with the ground.

But the trench was now a soggy pit brimming with brown-frothed rainwater. If we backed into it, we would have a major problem getting the vehicle out. With a herd of highly disturbed elephants inside, however, it was a risk we had to take.

What a disaster! The trench was too deep, and the trailer's sliding door jammed into the ground. To make matters worse, it was two a.m., pitch-black, and the rain was still coming down hard. I put out an emergency wake-up call to everyone on the reserve. Armed with shovels we slithered around in the sludge to hack a groove for the door.

Finally the big moment arrived. We all stood back, ready for the animals to be released into their new home.

However, as it had been an extremely stressful few hours, Kobus decided first to inject the herd with a mild sedative. With a pole-size syringe, he climbed onto the roof of the trailer. The roof had a large opening covered with slats that let air into the truck.

David jumped up to give him a hand. As soon as he landed on the roof, a trunk whipped through the slats as fast as a mamba snake and lashed at his ankle. David leapt back. He dodged the grasping trunk with a second to spare. If the elephant had caught him, he would have been yanked inside to a gruesome death. A person pulled into a confined space with seven angry elephants would soon be hamburger meat.

Thankfully everything went smoothly after that. As soon as the injections were administered and the elephants calmed down, we slid the truck door open. The new matriarch emerged. As the vehicles' headlights threw huge shadows on the trees behind, she tentatively stepped onto Thula Thula soil.

The six others followed. They were the new matriarch's baby bull; three females, one of whom was an adult; an eleven-year-old bull; and, the last out, the fifteen-year-old, three-and-half-ton teenage son of the previous matriarch. He walked a few yards and even in his groggy state realized there were humans behind him. He swiveled his head around and stared at us. Then he flared his ears and, with a high-pitched trumpet of rage, turned and charged. He stopped just short of slamming into the fence in front of us. He instinctively knew, even at his tender age, that he must protect the herd.

I smiled with absolute admiration. His mother and baby sister had been shot before his eyes. He had been darted and confined in a trailer for eighteen hours. But here he was, just a teenager, defending his family. David immediately named him "Mnumzane" (pronounced *nom-zahn*), which in Zulu means "sir."

We christened the new matriarch "Nana," which is what all Anthony grandchildren call my mom, Regina Anthony, a respected matriarch in her own right.

Nana, the matriach.

The second female in command, the most feisty, we called "Frankie" after Françoise. The other names would come later.

Nana gathered her clan, loped up to the fence, and stretched out her trunk to touch the electric wires. The 8,000-volt wires sent a jolt shuddering through her hulk. Whoa . . . she hurriedly backed off. Then, with her family in tow, she strode the entire perimeter of the *boma*, with her trunk curled fractionally below the wire to sense the current's pulse. She was checking for the weakest link as she must have seen her sister, the previous matriarch, do.

I watched, barely breathing. Nana completed the check and, smelling the watering hole, led her herd off to drink.

The most important part of having an electrified *boma* is fine-tuning how long you keep the animals inside. Too short, and they don't learn enough to respect the mega-volt punch the fence packs. Too long, and they somehow figure out that it's possible to endure the painful convulsions for the few seconds it takes to snap the electric wires—like the previous matriarch did. Once that happens they will never fear electricity again.

Unfortunately no one knows exactly what that perfect amount of time is. Opinions vary from a few days for more calm elephants to three months for wilder ones. My new herd was anything but calm. How long I should pen them was anybody's guess. What the experts had told me, however, was that during the quarantine period the animals should have no contact with humans. So once the gates were bolted, I instructed everyone to move off except for two game guards who would watch from a distance.

As we were leaving, I noticed the elephants lining up at a corner of the fence. They were facing due north, the exact direction of their former home. It was as if their inner compasses were telling them something.

It looked ominous.

8

One morning soon after, I awoke to a pounding on my door. I heard Ndonga yelling, "The elephants have gone! They've broken out of the *boma*! They've gone!"

I leapt out of bed, yanked on my trousers, and stumbled on one leg.

"I'm coming. Hang on!" I shouted.

An agitated Ndonga was outside, shivering in the pre-dawn chill.

"The two big ones started shoving a tree," he said. "They worked as a team, pushing it until it crashed down on the fence. The wires shorted out, and the elephants smashed through. Just like that."

Dread slithered in my belly. "What tree?"

"You know, that tambouti. The one that KZN Wildlife said was too big to pull down."

That tree must have weighed several tons and was thirty feet tall. Yet Nana and Frankie had figured out that by working together they could topple it. Despite my dismay, I felt a flicker of pride. These were some animals, all right.

We had to move fast. We had a massive crisis on our

hands. The herd was stampeding toward the border fence. If they broke through it, they would run straight into the patch-work of rural homes scattered outside Thula Thula. And, as any game ranger will say, a herd of wild elephants on the run in a populated area is the conservation equivalent of a nuclear disaster.

Within minutes we had a search party gathered at the *boma*. The large tambouti tree was history. Its toppled upper section was barely connected to the splintered stump by a strip of bark that was oozing poisonous sap. The fence looked as though several tanks had thundered through it.

The astounded Ovambo guard who had witnessed the breakout was standing next to the shattered tree. He pointed us in the direction he had last seen the elephants heading.

We quickly followed the spoor to the boundary, but we were too late. The border fence was down. The elephants had broken out.

Judging by their tracks, they had reached the fence, milled around for a while, and then backtracked into the reserve until—unbelievably—they found the energizer that powers the fence. How they knew that this small, ordinary machine hid-den in a thicket half a mile away was the source of the fence's electric current baffled us. But somehow they did. They tram-pled it like a tin can and returned to the boundary, where the wires were now dead. They then shouldered the concrete-embedded poles out of the ground as if they were matchsticks.

Their tracks pointed north. There was no doubt that they were on their way home to Mpumalanga, six hundred miles away. Even though it was a home that no longer wanted them, it was the only home they knew. In all probability, they would be shot upon arrival. That was assuming game rangers or hunters didn't get them along the way first.

As daybreak filled the eastern sky, a motorist three miles away spotted the herd loping up the road toward him. At first he thought he was seeing things. Elephants? There aren't any elephants here. . . .

Half a mile or so later, he saw the flattened fence and put two and two together. Fortunately, he had the presence of mind to call us. He gave us valuable information.

The chase was on. I gunned my Land Rover into gear, and the trackers leapt into the back.

We had barely driven out of the reserve when, to my astonishment, we saw a group of men parked on the shoulder of the dirt road. They were dressed in khaki and camouflage hunting gear and carrying rifles. You could feel their excitement.

I stopped and got out of the vehicle. The trackers and David were behind me.

"What're you guys doing?"

One looked at me, his eyes darting with anticipation.

"We're going after elephants."

"Oh yeah? Which ones?"

"They've bust out of Thula, man. We're gonna shoot them before they kill someone—they're fair game now."

I stared at him for several seconds, grappling to absorb this new twist to my problems. Then cold fury set in.

"Those elephants belong to me," I said, taking two paces

forward to emphasize my point. "If you put a bullet anywhere near them, you are going to have to deal with me. And when we're finished, I'm going to sue you."

I paused, breathing deeply.

"Now show me your hunting permit," I demanded, knowing he couldn't possibly have obtained one before dawn.

He stared at me, his face reddening with belligerence.

"They've escaped, okay? They can be legally shot. We don't need your permission."

David was standing next to me, his fists clenched. I could sense his outrage. "You know, David," I said loudly, "just look at this lot. Out there is a herd of confused elephants in big trouble and we're the only ones here without guns. We're the only ones who don't want to kill them. Shows the difference in priorities, doesn't it?"

Fizzing with anger, I ordered my men back into the Land Rover. Revving the engine and churning up dust clouds for the benefit of the gunmen staring at us aggressively, we sped up the road.

The encounter shook me up. Technically they were correct. The elephants *were* fair game. We had just heard on our two-way radios that the KZN Wildlife authorities, whom we alerted as soon as the herd had broken out, were issuing elephant rifles to their staff. I didn't have to be told that they were considering shooting the animals on sight. Their prime concern was the safety of people in the area, and no one could blame them.

For us, it was now a simple race against time. We had to find the elephants before anyone with a gun did.

9

One mile up the road, the herd's tracks veered into the bush, exactly as the motorist had told us. Thula Thula is flanked by vast forests of acacia trees and *ugagane* bush, which grows thickly with interwoven, thorn-studded branches that are like whips. The wickedly sharp thorns scarcely scratch an elephant's hide, but to us soft-skinned species, it is the equivalent of running through a maze of fishhooks.

The forest spread north as far as the eye could see. Could we find the animals in this dense wilderness? For us to have a fighting chance of catching the elephants before some gunman did, we had to have a helicopter tracking them from above. But to get a chopper would cost thousands of dollars, with no guarantee of success. Also, most commercial pilots wouldn't have a clue how to scout elephants hiding in such rugged terrain.

But there was one man I knew who could track from the sky. Peter Bell was, among other things, an expert game-capture pilot, not to mention a good man to have on your side in an emergency. I quickly drove back to Thula Thula and phoned him.

Peter didn't have to be told how serious the problem

was. Without a minute's hesitation, he agreed to help. While he got his chopper ready, we continued the chase on foot. But we had barely entered the acacia jungle when our Ovambo game guards, staring at what appeared to me to be a flinty patch of dirt, shook their heads. After some discussion, they proclaimed that the elephants had turned back.

"Are you sure?" I asked the head tracker.

He nodded and pointed toward Thula Thula. "They have turned. They are going that way."

This was news I was desperate to hear. Perhaps they would voluntarily return to the reserve. After twenty minutes of some of the toughest going I have ever experienced, however, I began to have doubts. Sweat was cascading down my face as I called over the chief tracker.

"The elephants are not here," I said. "There is no spoor, no dung, and no broken branches. No signs at all."

He shook his head, as if patiently talking to a child, and pointed ahead. "They are there."

Against my better judgment we carried on a bit farther and then I had enough. There was something wrong here. It was obvious there were no elephants around. An elephant, because of its massive size and strength, leaves very clear tracks, piles of dung, and snapped branches.

I called David, Ngwenya, and Bheki and told the Ovambos they were wrong. We were returning to the original tracks. The Ovambos shrugged but made no move to join us. I was too wrapped up in the intensity of the chase to think much about that at the time.

An hour later, we picked up fresh spoor that was heading in completely the opposite direction. Why had the Ovambos chosen the wrong route? Had they led me the wrong way on purpose? Surely not . . . I could only guess that they were scared of stumbling, without warning, upon the elephants in this wild terrain.

We kept in radio contact with Peter, who flew tight search grids over the bush ahead while John Tinley, a KZN Wildlife ranger from our neighboring reserve called Fundimvelo, visited nearby settlements asking headmen if any of their people had seen the herd. The answer was no, which was good news. Our biggest concern was that the animals would wander into a village and stomp on thatched huts. Or, worse, kill people.

10

Hot and scratched, shirts dark with sweat, and our nerves jangling, we kept moving. Every now and then we found signs that confirmed we were on the right track. I reckoned we were at least two hours behind them, but they could have been just ahead, waiting in ambush. That fear was always with us. More than once we froze, our hearts in our mouths until a kudu or a bushbuck burst out of the thick bush in a crackle of snapping sticks.

Our progress was torturously slow, but it was impossible to move faster. Thorns parted as one man squeezed through a gap, and then snapped back at the man behind.

For us to catch up to the elephants, they would need to stop to rest somewhere, like a watering hole. A factor in our favor was that they had Nana's two-year-old son in tow. He would slow them down significantly. Or so I hoped. (We later named this little one *Mandla*, the Zulu word for "power," in honor of his incredible stamina in staying with the herd during this long chase.)

After a long, hot, thirsty, and frustrating day, the sun dipped below the horizon and we stopped. Nobody stumbles around a thorny jungle at night looking for elephants. Tracking the animals in the thick stuff during daylight is bad enough. In the dark it's suicide.

Reluctantly I called off the search for the day. Back home, Max flopped at my feet, his tail thumping on the floor. He seemed to sense my dismay and nudged me with his wet nose. Stroking his broad head, I mulled over the events of the day. What had possessed the herd to smash through two electrified fences? Why had the Ovambos made such a careless mistake with their tracking? Why had they then abandoned the search?

There was something that didn't gel.

Max's low growl jerked me out of my thoughts. I looked down. He was fully alert, head up, ears half cocked, staring into the dark.

Then a soft voice called out: "Mkhulu."

Mkhulu is my Zulu name. It literally means "grandfather." Zulus respect maturity, and to refer to someone as a *Mkhulu* was a compliment.

It was Bheki.

"*Sawubona*," I said, giving the traditional greeting. *I see you.*

"*Yebo*." Yes, he nodded and paused for a while, as if thinking over what he wanted to say next.

"Mkhulu, there is a mystery here. People are making big trouble.

"A gun spoke next to the *boma* last night," he continued, "and the elephants were shouting and calling. They were crazy. Maybe one was even shot."

"*Hau!*" I used the Zulu exclamation for surprise. "But how do you know such important things?"

"I was there," he replied. "I know the elephants are valuable, so I stayed near to the *boma* last night, watching. I don't trust the *amagweragwer.*" The word means "foreigners," but I knew he was referring to the Ovambo guards, who were from Namibia.

"Then the big females came together and pushed a tree onto the fence," Bheki went on. "There was much force and it fell hard and broke the fence and they went out. They were running. I was afraid because they came close past me."

"Thank you very much," I said. "You have done well."

Satisfied that his message had been delivered, Bheki stepped back into the darkness.

I exhaled loudly. Now that would explain a lot, I thought, my mind racing. A poacher shooting next to the *boma* unaware of the elephants' presence would certainly have put the jitters into the herd, particularly as their previous matriarch and baby had been shot barely forty-eight hours ago.

But as much as I liked Bheki, I treated his suspicions about the Ovambo guards with caution. Hostility between ethnic groups in Africa often runs deep, and I knew there was little love lost between the Zulus and the Namibians. There was a possibility that the Zulu staff might use the confusion surrounding the escape to get the Ovambos in trouble, so other Zulus could get their jobs.

However, Bheki had certainly provided food for thought.

11

At dawn, we drove to where we had left off the day before. The tracking team plunged back into the thorny bush to pick up the spoor on the ground. I decided to go with Peter and track from the air. As the chopper rose, I gazed out over the stretch of Africa below us. It was so steeped in history. It was once home to every kind of wild African animal—until most of them were over-hunted, some to extinction. Many of the ones that remained were endangered.

Now conservationists were making a stand. The key was to involve local communities in the benefits of and profits to be had from conservation and ecotourism. It was often hard, frustrating work to convince people, but it was a struggle that had to be fought and won. Tribal cooperation was the key to Africa's conservation health. We neglected that at everyone's peril.

We flew north along the Nseleni River. It was difficult to see much because the lush growth could have hidden a tank.

Then at last, we got some news. KZN Wildlife radioed that they had received a report of a sighting. The herd had chased a group of boys tending cows off a watering hole the previous afternoon. Fortunately there had been no casualties.

We now had a confirmed position for the elephants. Peter dropped me near the team, and I jumped into the waiting Land Rover.

Me coordinating the search effort.

Then we got another call from KZN Wildlife. The elephants had changed direction and were heading toward the Umfolozi game reserve. Umfolozi was KZN Wildlife's main sanctuary about twenty miles from Thula Thula. KZN gave us an estimated location, which we radioed to the chopper.

Peter found the herd in the early afternoon, just a few miles from Umfolozi's fence. This was some distance from our position on the ground. The elephants were moving along steadily, and Peter knew he had to force them around before they broke into Umfolozi. He would be unable to get them back once they were within the reserve's fences.

There is only one way to herd elephants from the air, and

it's not pretty. You have to fly straight at the animals until they turn and move in the opposite direction. In this case, we needed them to turn back toward Thula Thula.

Peter banked and then whirred down. The chopper's blades clattered and came straight at Nana. They skimmed just above her head before making a tight U-turn. Then the chopper came back from the same angle. It hovered in front of the animals to block them from going forward.

This is stomach-churning stuff. It requires top-level flying skills, rock-steady hands, and even steadier nerves. If you fly too high, the elephants will slip through underneath and be gone. If you fly too low, you risk hitting trees.

At this stage, the elephants had been on the run for more than twenty-four hours. They were exhausted and should have turned wearily away from the giant chopper furiously buzzing at them. That is what 99 percent of animals would have done.

This herd stood firm.

Again and again the chopper came at them, yet Nana and her family refused to retreat. Their trunks curled in defiance whenever Peter came in low and close. But they didn't budge. He radioed to tell us what was happening, and I realized that my herd was something else. Maybe I was biased, but they were special.

Eventually, through superb flying, Peter managed to wear them down. Inch by inch he edged them around until they were finally facing Thula Thula. Then he got them moving, herding them from above, maneuvering his machine like a flying sheepdog.

12

I started to breathe easier and dared to believe that everything was going to be all right. Back at Thula Thula, workers had spent the day mending the ruined fences, both at the *boma* and the border. They radioed me to say everything was ready. We would have to cut open a section of fence to drive them through, but we wouldn't know where to cut until they arrived.

Finally, after hours of herding from the sky, we saw the helicopter hover low on the far horizon. They were almost there. I gave instructions to the fence team to drop a wide section of the fence to provide instant access into the reserve and prayed the frazzled matriarch would go straight in.

Then I caught sight of her for the first time. She was pushing slowly through the bush just below the thundering helicopter. All I could make out were the tips of her ears and the hump on her back, but it was the most welcome thing I have ever seen.

Soon they all came into view, plodding on until they were at the road. Just fifteen yards from the lowered fence, Nana tested the air with her trunk—and halted.

The mood suddenly changed. Instead of tired acceptance, the herd was now filled with defiance. Nana trumpeted her belligerence and drew her family close in the classic defensive position. They stood with their bottoms together facing outward, like the spokes of a wheel, and they held their ground with grim determination. Peter buzzed them continuously, goading them to make that last little sprint into the reserve. But to no avail.

Seeing he was getting nowhere, Peter peeled off and landed. Leaving the chopper's motor running, he sprinted over to me.

"I don't like to do this," he said, "but the only thing left is to go up and fire shots behind them. Force them to move forward. Can I borrow your gun?"

"No, I don't like it—"

"Lawrence," Peter interrupted, "we have spent a lot of time on this and I can't come back tomorrow. It's now or never. You decide."

Gunfire was last thing I wanted. It meant more shooting around the already traumatized creatures.

But Peter was right. I had run out of alternatives. I unholstered my pistol and handed it to him.

Peter took it without a word, lifted off in the chopper, and hovered just behind the animals. He started firing rapid shots into the ground. *Crack, crack, crack.*

He might as well have used spitballs. They didn't move. This was where they were going to make their stand. This was their line in the sand.

Dusk fell, and in the glow of the stars I could see the shapes of the elephants, still holding firm.

I felt sick with despair. We had been so close to pulling it off. Peter banked and flew off. He radioed that it was too dark for him to land without lights and he would drop my gun off at Thula Thula.

Realizing their "persecutor" had left, Nana turned her bone-tired family around and they disappeared into the thick bush.

I groaned. Now we would have to do it all again—without a helicopter—the next day.

13

I was up before my four a.m. alarm rang, desperate to get going.

As the first shards of pink dawn pierced the darkness, we picked up the spoor of Nana and her family from the night before. Their tracks again pointed north toward the Umfolozi game reserve. We followed their new path through the thorny thickets, going as fast as we could. But the herd had a ten-hour lead on us.

Later that morning, I heard from KZN Wildlife that the elephants had broken into the Umfolozi reserve during the night at two different points several miles apart. They had crashed through the electric fence with ease because it was only live-wired from the inside.

The herd had split into two groups during the night, with Nana, her two calves, and Mnumzane in one group. Frankie and her son and daughter were in the other. They met up again only when they were deep in the reserve. The two groups traveled seven miles apart and then came together in the dense bush.

I thought this was remarkable. There is no doubt that

elephants possess incredible communication abilities. We know they emit rumblings at frequencies far below human hearing. They can detect those rumblings even when they're many miles apart from one another. Many scientists believe that the animals pick up the sounds with their huge ears. But there is a newer theory that they feel the vibrations through their feet. Whatever it is, these amazing creatures have some senses far superior to ours.

Close to where the two groups had reconnected, there was a thatched rondavel—a circular Zulu hut—that was used by KZN Wildlife anti-poaching units. The rangers inside were fast asleep when they felt the flimsy building shake. It must have felt like an earthquake had hit. Then the top half of the two-part door burst open, and in the moonlight they saw a trunk snake its way through. The elephants had smelled the rangers' sacks of cornmeal, a Zulu staple. They had decided to take their share, which, of course, meant all of it. The men scurried under their beds as the trunk weaved like a super-sized vacuum cleaner around the hut and yanked out the maize sacks.

Several other twisting trunks shattered the windows. The elephants reached in and smashed the furniture as they searched for more food. One man's bush jacket was wrenched from his hands. He peeked through the splintered door and saw the shadowy figures of young calves playfully stomping on it and flipping it into the air.

Not once did the men reach for their weapons. Their lives were devoted to saving animals. They would kill one only as a last resort. Shaken as they were, this was not that kind of situation.

As soon as the rampaging giants left, the rangers radioed the game reserve's headquarters.

At dawn, Umfolozi's conservation manager, Peter Hartley, decided to assess the situation. He spotted the animals in the distance and began to approach them cautiously on foot. He was still some distance away when Frankie swiveled. She had picked up his scent.

Elephants seldom charge humans unless they get too close. But, with a bellow of rage, Frankie thundered toward Peter. Caught by surprise, Peter turned and ran for his life through the thornveld, cutting himself as he scrambled through the razorlike bushes. He leapt into his vehicle and sped off with five tons of storming, crushing force just yards behind him.

I was still in the bush when I got a radio call that it was urgent for me to go to Umfolozi to meet with KZN Wildlife. While I was relieved that the elephants were safe for the moment, I was afraid I was about to hear their death sentences.

KZN Wildlife said exactly what I had dreaded. If they had known about the elephants' troubled background, they would never have granted the permit. The fact that the animals had broken through two electric fences, chased cattle, raided a guards' hut, resisted a buzzing helicopter, and charged Peter clearly indicated that this was a dangerous, unsettled herd. The risk of letting them remain in an area with rural settlements was too high.

This meant only one thing. The rangers were going to kill the herd.

I was determined not to let this happen. I argued that it was just bad luck that the herd had escaped. We had done everything by the book. As soon as I could get the elephants used to Thula Thula, I stressed, they would be okay. I also pointed out that they hadn't hurt any humans, despite being on the run for three days.

I begged for one more chance.

The rangers did not want to kill any animal unless it was absolutely unavoidable. They said that in this case they didn't think Nana and her family had much going for them. Hard experience had shown the rangers that there was little hope for any herd that refused to respect an electric fence.

I knew that what they were saying was true, but I still asked if we could get the elephants back to the *boma* and see if they calmed down. "If they're still out of control in a couple of months, then we'll have no choice," I stated in all seriousness. "I'll take full responsibility."

After what seemed like an eternity, they said they would think about it.

14

The next day, I got a call from a stranger who introduced himself as a wildlife dealer.

"I've heard about your elephant problem," he said. "And I may have the perfect solution."

"Like what?" I asked.

"I'll buy the herd. Lock, stock, and barrel. Not only that, I'll give you another one as a replacement. A good herd. Normal animals that won't give you any hassles."

"You mean circus elephants?" I couldn't keep the sarcasm from my voice.

"No, nothing like that. These are wild animals, just not as aggressive as yours. And I'll give you twenty thousand dollars."

"Why would you do that?"

"If your animals stay here, one way or another they will be shot. If I take them, they will be relocated to a sanctuary in Angola where there are no humans to worry them. At least they will be allowed to live."

That certainly shook me. Here was a man offering to solve my problems in one single stroke. I would recover my initial

costs of transporting the elephants and building the *boma*—
and I would get another herd for free. Considering that I also
was about to be hit with more capture and transport costs to
get my herd back to Thula Thula from the Umfolozi reserve,
it was quite an attractive offer. If I didn't accept it, I was going
to have to fork out a lot of cash.

"Give me your number and I'll get back to you," I said.

Something bothered me, though. Perhaps this was just
too good to be true. I have always followed my instincts, and
something didn't smell right about this.

In fact, the more I thought about the dealer, the more
irritated I became. The sane reaction would have been to be
grateful for the lifeline being offered. Instead, I felt strangely
annoyed.

Then it dawned on me. That phone call made me realize
that I had already forged a bond with this delinquent herd,
even though I barely knew them. And the strength of the
connection shocked me.

The past few days had shown me that, even with ecotourism, elephants didn't really count for much in the real world.
To hunters, they were target practice with a prize of ivory. To
the local people, they were a threat. To me, though, this was
a group of desperate and bewildered animals who had been
on the run. Yet no one cared about that or the fact that these
were animals whose ancestors had roamed this planet for
centuries.

Our urgent, three-day chase had hammered home to me
the reality that these immensely powerful giants were actually

as vulnerable as babies. Wherever this lost and confused group went, they would be at risk without someone fighting in their corner. As it was, Nana and Frankie were in all likelihood about to be executed.

Once I grasped that, an almost irrational link was established that would re-chart the course of my life. Like it or not, I felt part of the herd. Life had dealt them a cruel hand, and I was determined to fix what I could.

I owed them that at least.

15

Finally, after several depressing days, good news arrived. KZN Wildlife agreed that the elephants could return to Thula Thula. Nana and Frankie had been pardoned.

But if they escaped again, I was told, the entire herd would be shot on sight. And there would be no further discussion. This was no casual threat. I was told that Africa's infamous elephant rifle, the .458, was now being issued as standard equipment to all rangers in the area.

This was our last chance.

I spent most of the time waiting for the herd to be returned trying to figure out how to get the animals to calm down once they were back. Before I could let them out of the *boma* into the freedom of the greater reserve, I had to be absolutely certain they were settled. But how?

After a while, KZN Wildlife phoned to say the herd would be delivered the following day.

Elephant capture is done throughout South Africa, just

not in KwaZulu-Natal. The team at Umfolozi was famous for capturing and saving the white rhino from extinction. But they did not have the heavy equipment required for elephant herds. They did have, however, a new heavy trailer designed to transport either giraffes or a few elephants. Would it be strong and large enough for all seven elephants? Would the Umfolozi team be able to move the hefty creatures into the trailer without the specialized equipment used elsewhere? My elephants were going to be guinea pigs, so to speak.

I was comforted that my good friend Dave Cooper, Umfolozi's internationally respected wildlife veterinarian and probably the top rhino expert in the world, would be in charge of the elephants' welfare.

Capture always takes place early in the day to avoid heat stress on the animals. At six a.m., a helicopter carrying an experienced marksman with a tranquilizer gun flew off to find the herd. The goal was to turn the animals on the run in the direction we needed them to go.

When the pilot sighted the elephants, he brought the chopper down low until it hovered just above the ground. He made it sway this way, then that. He charged forward at the now-frantic elephants, herding them toward a dirt track several hundred yards ahead. The ground crew would be barreling down that road with the transport truck. The truck needed to be as close as possible to where the animals went down once they were tranquilized.

The marksman loaded the dart gun and readied himself as the pilot radioed his position to the ground crew.

The herd was now in full flight. They crashed through the bush with the clattering chopper blades egging them on.

Suddenly Nana, with family in tow, broke through the tree cover and into open ground at the area chosen for the darting.

The pilot deftly shifted to be just behind the stampeding animals. This offered the marksman a clear view of the elephants' broad backsides.

Crack! A hefty aluminum dart filled with M99, a powerful anesthetic customized for elephants, hit Nana's rump. The matriarch is always darted first, followed by the other larger animals. The calves are darted last to prevent them from being trampled or smothered by the larger family members. Nana's calf was, in fact, too small to dart safely from the air. So Dave was going to dart the calf on the ground.

Bright-red dart feathers stuck out of the rumps of the running animals. As soon as each dart hit its target, the marksman rapidly loaded and fired another one. He had to work quickly. Any delay between shots and there would be comatose elephants spread out all over the bush, which would complicate matters immeasurably.

Once the last dart hit its target, the marksman gave a thumbs-up, and the chopper gained altitude. First Nana, then the others staggered, sank to their knees, and collapsed in slow motion.

The ground team's speeding trucks arrived right on time. Dave hurried to where Nana lay in the dirt. Her baby, Mandla, was standing nervously next to his mother's fallen body. He flapped his ears and reared his tiny trunk, instinctively trying to protect her. Dave got into position and fired a light plastic dart loaded with the smallest effective dose into the baby's shoulder.

As Mandla's knees folded, the vet broke a twig off a nearby tree and placed it inside the end of Nana's trunk to keep the airways open. He did the same to the other elephants, and then went back to Nana. He squeezed ointment into her exposed pupil, then pulled her huge ear over her eye to protect it from the sun.

The other slumbering beasts got the same treatment, and he methodically checked each one for injuries. Fortunately none had fallen awkwardly. There were no broken bones or torn ligaments.

The ground team arrived and immediately reversed the transport truck up to Nana. As the matriarch, they wanted her loaded first. This was done by winching her into the air feetfirst. Then they deposited her at the rear entrance of the truck. There, Nana was pulled and pushed into the truck by teams of men, and she was revived by Dave with an injection of M5050.

A five-ton elephant—all muscle, blood, and bone—hanging upside down is not a pretty sight. But the job was done as gently and rapidly as possible. Without specialized equipment, however, the process took much longer than normal. While the larger animals were being laboriously loaded, the effects of the drug started to wear off in some of those waiting their turn.

When a drugged elephant starts to wake up, you don't waste time. As trunks started to twitch and elephants attempted to raise their heads, Dave ran from one to the next. He injected additional drugs to each one through a large vein in the ear.

Once the entire herd was onboard and awake, the truck sped off to Thula Thula. The animals recovered during the ninety-minute journey, and although a little wobbly, Nana led her family back into the *boma*. She was followed by Frankie, who looked as defiant as ever. Their bid for freedom had, if anything, increased their resentment of captivity. I knew we would have a rough few months ahead of us.

16

As the capture team drove off, one game ranger shouted over his shoulder, "See you soon!"

This was no polite good-bye. His meaning was clear. He was saying these animals were bad news. He had no doubt that the herd would break out again and he would be back. But the next time it would be with bullets, not darts. I was too angry to think of a comeback quickly enough.

The next day, the wildlife dealer phoned again. Now he doubled his offer to forty thousand dollars. Again, I stalled. I couldn't shake the belief that fate had sent me these elephants, and that maybe some things were meant to be.

Just before nightfall, I drove to the *boma*. Nana was standing in thick cover with her family behind her. She watched my every move, meanness seeping from her every pore. There was absolutely no doubt that sooner or later they were going to make another break for it.

I decided then and there that I would go and live with them. I knew the experts would be horrified by this idea. We had been repeatedly instructed that to keep the elephants wild, human contact must be kept to the barest minimum.

And I knew this herd had already had too much human contact—and the very worst kind. Their rehabilitation, if such a thing was even possible, called for uncommon measures. Since I was responsible for this last-ditch effort to save their lives, I needed to do things my way.

I would remain outside the *boma*, of course, but I would stay with them, feed them, talk to them, and most important, be with them day and night. These magnificent creatures were extremely distressed and disorientated and maybe, just maybe, if someone who cared about them was constantly with them, they would have a chance. There was no doubt that unless we tried something different, they would break out again and die.

It boiled down to this: We had to get to know each other or else all bets were off. We had to get the matriarch to trust at least one person. Unless that happened, the herd would always be suspicious of humans and would never settle down.

The *boma* was about three miles away from my house. With Françoise's blessing, my game ranger David and I packed the Land Rover with basic supplies. The vehicle would be our home for as long as it took. I also brought Max, who was great company outdoors. I knew he would behave around the elephants.

We would be with the elephants around the clock, living in the bush, catnapping in the truck or stretching out under the stars with our wristwatch alarms set to remind us to patrol the fences. We would share the cold nights with them, and we would sweat together in the searingly hot days. It would be mentally and physically exhausting—especially because the herd had clearly let us know that they didn't want us around.

17

The first day we watched the herd from a distance of about thirty yards. Nana and Frankie watched us back. They rushed up to the fence if they thought we were getting too close.

That night David's whisper woke me. "Quick. Something's happening at the fence." I threw off my blanket and blinked to adjust my eyes to night vision. We crept up to the *boma* through the bush. I saw nothing. Then an enormous shape loomed in front of me.

It was Nana. She was about ten yards from the fence. Mandla, her baby son, was next to her.

I strained my eyes, searching for the others. Despite their bulk, elephants are difficult enough to see in dense bush during the day, let alone at night. Then I saw them. They were all standing motionless in the dark just a little bit behind Nana.

I glanced at my watch. It was four forty-five a.m.

Suddenly Nana tensed her enormous frame and flared her ears.

Nana took a step forward. "Here she goes!" said David, no longer whispering. "That electric wire better hold."

Without thinking, I stood and walked toward the fence. Nana was directly ahead, a colossus just a few yards in front of me.

"Don't do it, Nana," I said, as calmly as I could. "Please don't do it, girl."

She stood motionless but tense, like a runner waiting for the start of a race. Behind her, the rest of the herd froze.

"This is your home now," I continued. "Please don't do it, girl."

Even though I could barely make out her face, I felt her eyes bore into me.

"They will kill you all if you break out," I explained. "This is your home now. You don't have to run anymore."

The absurdity of the situation struck me. Here I was in thick darkness talking, as if we were having a friendly chat, to a wild female elephant with a baby. It does not get more dangerous than that.

Still, I decided to continue. I meant every word and needed Nana to understand what I was saying. "You will all die if you go. Stay here. I will be here with you, and it's a good place."

Nana took a step forward. I could see her tense up, preparing to go all the way. If she could take the pain and snap the electric wire, the rest of the fence wouldn't hold. She would be out. Frankie and the rest would smash through after her in a flash.

I was well aware that I was directly in their path. The fence cables would hold them for a short while, but I would have only seconds to scramble out of their way and climb a tree, or else I would be stomped flatter than an envelope. The nearest tree, a big acacia robusta with sharp thorns, was perhaps ten yards to my left. I wondered if I would be fast enough. Possibly not. And when was the last time I had climbed a thorny tree?

Then something happened. Between Nana and me. For the briefest second, I felt a tiny spark of recognition from her.

It was gone as quickly as it came. Nana nudged Mandla with her trunk. They turned and melted into the bush. The rest followed.

David gave a mighty exhale. "I thought she was going for it," he said.

We lit a small fire and brewed coffee. I could not tell David that I thought I had connected for an instant with the matriarch; it would have sounded too crazy.

But something had happened.

18

Each day that followed was the same. As the sun came up, the herd would start pacing up and down the length of the fence. They turned and charged at us if we dared to get too close. They stopped right at the electric wire. Pure aggression and agitation—the fiercest I have seen from any animal—blazed nonstop whenever we approached the fence. And they would glare at us ferociously as we backed off to watch them from a distance.

Because they were in a confined area, we had to provide the herd with extra food. This posed a problem because whenever we tried to get close enough to the fence to throw bales of alfalfa into the enclosure, they ignored the food and exploded in fits of rage.

So I distracted the elephants at one side of the *boma* while David tossed bulky bales over the fence on the other side. As soon as they spotted him, they would turn and charge in his direction. He would back off, and I would throw food over from my side. Then they would come at me, and David would continue. The elephants would eat only when we moved well away.

There was no doubt that, in their fury, they would have

killed us if not for the fence—their hatred for people was so intense. I began to wonder what had happened to these creatures, especially since Marion had told me that when they were babies, Nana and Frankie had had some human contact. As far as I knew, they hadn't been physically mistreated, so was it something deeper? Was it some learned fear passed down from their ancestors who had been hunted to the brink? Was it because they instinctively knew humans were responsible for their confinement? Was it that because of us they could no longer stride the great migration trails across the continent as their ancestors had? Or was the death of their previous matriarch the final straw?

I spent the rest of the day just watching them, trying to pick up some vibe other than rage. It now seemed that Frankie, the second-in-command, was the main aggressor. Nana was fractionally calmer. Could I get through to her? I didn't know. I just hoped.

David and I were pushing up to two thousand pounds of food a day over the wire. In a week alone, we each lost ten pounds, most of it in sweat. If I hadn't been so worried, I would have relished being in such good shape.

One thing was certain. The elephants always knew David and I were around. I spent hours walking around the *boma*, checking the fence and deliberately speaking loudly so they heard my voice. If I ever caught Nana's attention, I would look directly at her and focus on positive, gentle communication. I told her time and time again that this was her family's new home and that everything she would ever need was here. Most of the day, though, I spent sitting or standing still at a chosen spot near the fence. I purposefully ignored them. I was just there doing nothing, saying nothing, showing I was comfortable whether they were close by or not.

Slowly but surely, we became part of their lives. They began to "know" us, but whether that was a good or bad thing, I still wasn't sure.

Every morning at precisely four forty-five a.m., they seemed most determined to break out. It became an alarming ritual. Nana would line up the herd facing toward their old home in Mpumalanga. She would then tense, yards from the fence, and for ten adrenaline-soaked minutes I would stand up to her and plead with her for their lives, telling her that this was now their home.

A close-up of Mabula, Frankie's son. Being face-to-face with an elephant in distress is very dangerous.

The words I used were unimportant as Nana obviously didn't understand English. I just concentrated on keeping my tone as reassuring as I could. It was always touch-and-go, and I was always tremendously relieved when she ghosted back into the bush with her family.

When the sun rose, David and I went back to the truck. We were shattered by these tense standoffs, saturated in sweat even in the early-morning chill.

Silently David would start a small fire near the Land Rover and put the coffeepot on, while each of us wondered what the day would bring. Why were they always so aggressive, even while we were giving them food? Why did they hate us so much? Elephants are intelligent creatures. Surely they must know by now that we meant no harm? I could understand them wanting to escape. Maybe I too would be frantic at being locked up . . . but this was something else.

I was starting to wonder whether we would ever settle them. Their hatred was so intense that perhaps the barriers between us were impassable. Maybe too much damage had already been done.

I just didn't know.

19

Nana and Frankie still regularly toppled trees toward the fence, but the ones close enough to do any damage had all been felled. However, there was a particularly tall acacia in a thicket some distance away that they started working on. Initially I didn't worry too much, as it seemed too far from the electric barrier. But when it crashed down, it "bounced" and some of the top branches snagged the wires and strained them to the breaking point.

This caused an electrical short with lots of crackling, which, fortunately, frightened the elephants off. Even better, the wires didn't snap, so there was still current. But the elephants would soon sense that this was a weak link and launch an assault. All they had to do was bump the fallen tree forward. The wires would give, and there would be no stopping the herd.

We had to act quickly. We examined all options but it soon became crystal clear that there was only one solution: Someone had to sneak into the *boma* with a saw and hack the branches off the fence.

David volunteered to do it. This was something I had never heard of being done before: a person going into a sealed electrified enclosure with seven wild elephants and no quick escape route.

I anguished for an hour or so. Could I be sending David to his death?

I came up with a plan and then decided we would go over all the steps again and again, until we had it right. David's life depended on it.

First, we would miss a feed. Once the elephants were really hungry, we would throw bales of alfalfa over the side of the *boma* farthest from the tree to keep the animals occupied as far away from David as possible.

Second, I would place two rangers with radios at the energizers to control the current. The power would be switched off at exactly the moment David was ready to climb in. As soon as he was in the *boma*, the electricity had to be turned back on, otherwise the animals might sense the power cut and break out while we were working. This, of course, would leave David trapped with 8,000 volts imprisoning him with the elephants.

Third, a ranger would be with me as my "communicator" to relay instructions and operate my radio. I would have the rifle, ready to shoot if David's life was unquestionably threatened.

We went over this several times, until we were as prepared as we would ever be. I gave the signal, and the rangers started heaving food over the fence to entice the herd and hopefully keep them engrossed long enough for David to finish the job.

As Nana led her hungry charges to the food bonanza, I looked at David. "You still want to do this?"

He shrugged. "If I don't, we'll lose them."

"Okay," I said, sweating at the mere thought of the enormous risk he was taking.

I nodded to the ranger next to me, who picked up his radio and shouted to the energizer crew, "Power off—go!"

David scaled the fence. Once he was in, I threw over the saw and gave the order, "Power on—now!"

The switches went up. David was now caged inside the *boma*.

I loaded the rifle, steadied the barrel on the Land Rover's open door, and zeroed in the sights on the elephants.

David had his back to the herd and was sawing the offending branches with quick-pumping arms while I gave a running commentary from over the rifle sights. "Everything's okay. No problem, no problem. It's working. You are doing fine; it's a piece of cake. Just a few more moments . . ."

In the blink of an eye, everything changed. Frankie, who was slightly behind the rest of the herd, must have heard a noise. She suddenly looked up. Enraged that someone was in her territory, she broke into a charge—as fast and deadly as a missile.

"David, get out! Now! Cut the power! Cut the power! Now! Now! She's coming!" I yelled.

But the message didn't get through to the rangers at the energizer. The drama of the charge had mesmerized the radioman next to me. He froze, completely stunned by the dreadful but magnificent sight of an elephant in full charge.

David was trapped with Frankie hurtling at him like a rocket. He clambered wildly over the felled tree and grabbed at the fence as five tons of enraged elephant thundered up at an impossible speed. He only had seconds to escape.

With my heart in my boots, I swore and took aim. I knew it was too late—everything had gone horribly wrong. I would put a bullet in Frankie's brain, but she was speeding at over thirty miles an hour; dead or alive, her momentum would smash into David and he would be pulverized. No creature alive can survive being hit by an elephant.

My trigger finger tightened, and in the microsecond that I was about to squeeze it, I heard the foulest language you could imagine.

It was David! He was right next to me, cursing the radio-man who hadn't relayed the "cut power" message. I jerked the rifle up as Frankie broke off and bolted past us, trunk high, ears flaring, turning tightly to avoid the wires.

Slowly, I lowered the rifle and stared at David, dumbstruck. He had just scaled an eight-foot-high electrical fence. But he was shaking with anger, not an overdose of electricity.

I know plenty of stories of people doing impossible things in dangerous situations, but 8,000 volts will smack you flat on your back no matter how much your adrenaline is pumping. It's got enough juice to stop a multi-ton creature. You don't get bigger league than that.

Yet David had done it. Against all odds, it seems he some-how missed touching all four of the prominent live wires in his frantic scramble for safety. How, none of us would ever know.

But one thing is certain. If David had been hurled back-ward by the shock, Frankie would have been on him, whether I killed her or not. She was too close and too fast. Nothing could have saved him.

As soon as everyone calmed down, David insisted on climbing back into the *boma* and finishing the job. Afterward, we drove up to the main house for a much-needed break.

Later that night, David and I returned to the elephants. We inspected the *boma* and catnapped for a few hours in the Land Rover. At four forty-five a.m., I heard a slight rustle near the fence. With dread I knew it was Nana preparing for her predawn breakout attempt, as she did every morning. I walked down, by now knowing exactly where she would be. Once again, Mandla was at her side. The rest of the herd was lined up behind them.

"Please don't do it, girl," I said.

Nana stopped, tense as a spring as she watched me. I kept using her name as I urged her to stay, speaking as low and persuasively as I could.

Suddenly she shifted to face me head-on. Her furious stare faded for a moment. Instead, something else flickered in her eyes. It wasn't necessarily friendliness, but it wasn't hostility, either.

"This is your home now, Nana," I repeated. "It's a good home and I will always be here with you."

With unhurried dignity, Nana turned away from the fence. The others moved to let her through and then followed closely behind her.

After a few yards she stopped and let the others go ahead. She had never done that before. She had always been the first to disappear into the bush. She turned and again looked straight at me.

It was only a few seconds, but it seemed to go on forever.

Then she was swallowed up by the darkness.

20

When we first started to live with the herd, the wildlife outside the *boma* wanted to know who we were, what we were, and what we were doing on their turf. Wherever we went, hundreds of eyes watched. I had that prickly sensation of being under constant surveillance. Whenever I looked up, a mongoose, warthog, or tawny eagle would be peering at us from a distance, not missing anything we did.

Soon we too were considered to be creatures of the wild. The larger animals got used to us and sensed we posed no danger. So they started to move freely around us. The resident impala ram and his herd, normally skittish, grazed thirty or so paces away, as if we were part of the scenery. Zebra and wildebeest came past regularly, while kudu and nyala browsed nearby, completely at ease.

But that didn't mean we were entirely welcome. A troop of baboons complained bitterly as they sauntered past on their daily trip to the river. We had unknowingly camped slap in the middle of their domain, and they had no hesitation in expressing their disapproval. Sitting on top of a Natal mahogany tree, the troop leader showed his dagger-shaped yellow teeth and snarled, *HOOH, HOOH, HAAA*, across the valley. *BOH, BOH,* his deep territorial call echoed down the riverbed. To him, we would always be trespassers.

It was late spring, and birds of all shapes and sizes, feathered in an explosion of African colors, chirped and sang the stories of their lives to all who would listen. Snakes, including the lethal black mamba, sought shade from the baking sun. My favorite snake was a beautiful rock python that lived in a group of boulders beside a gully. He was still a youngster, less than five feet long, but I thought watching his olive-and-tan body rippling over the ground was as special as you could get.

A one-inch bark spider we named Wilma took up residence on the Land Rover's two-way radio antenna. Despite her small size, Wilma was an absolute dynamo. Every evening she wove a new three-yard-wide web on the antenna. The web was an engineering marvel. It was a super-sticky trap that held fast any insect unlucky enough to fly into it, including four-inch longhorn beetles. Wilma methodically sucked the life out of them. Then every morning, she gobbled up the web.

Sometimes we needed to go to the far end of the *boma*, but when we started the vehicle, Wilma clung on to her just-completed web in a flat panic. In the end, we always took pity on her and walked instead.

At dusk, animals that lived in the sun went off to sleep wherever they felt safest. The landscape emptied, but not for long. It was soon repopulated under the light of the African stars by creatures of the night. Warthogs gave way to bush pigs. Tawny and martial eagles were replaced by giant eagle owls that scouted the skies on silent wings and swooped down on vondos—plump, oversize bush rats. Fiery-necked nightjars snatched insects in mid-flight. Thousands upon thousands of bats scudded through the air, and bushbabies, among the cutest creatures alive with their cuddly-looking little bodies and huge eyes, screeched from the treetops.

Hyenas, among my favorite animals, skulked in the alleys of the dark looking for dinner. *YOOUP YOOUP, YOOOOUP,* they called, marking their territory with their manic cackles. Sometimes in the morning, we saw huge doglike footprints nearby. Apparently during the night they would come in for a closer look at us.

We watched all these animals with the spotlight but didn't keep it on for too long. It's bad bush practice to keep a light on continuously. Light attracts insects, insects attract frogs, and frogs attract snakes. Our only ongoing light was the campfire.

One morning, we woke to find leopard droppings near the Land Rover. The local male had marked his territory right where we were sleeping. He had delivered a firm feline message: This was also his space.

Our location gave me plenty of time to study the elephant herd. As the weeks passed, I could see them gradually start to settle down. We were now able to approach the fence at feeding time without being charged by enraged elephants. And I became fascinated by their individual quirks.

Nana, huge and dominant, took her matriarchal duties seriously. She used every inch of the *boma* to the maximum. She marked out the best spots for shade and the best shelter from the wind. Somehow she also knew feeding times to the minute. And she knew exactly when the watering hole and mud pond were due to be refilled by us.

Frankie was the herd's self-appointed guardian. She delighted in breaking away from the rest to storm past us at full speed with her head held high, glaring fiercely for no reason at all.

Mandla, Nana's baby boy, was a born clown whose antics kept us endlessly amused. He would regularly mock-charge us—as long as his mom was close by.

Frankie and Mabula.

Mabula and Marula, Frankie's thirteen-year-old son and eleven-year-old daughter, were always quiet and well behaved. They seldom strayed far from their mother.

Nandi, Nana's teenage daughter and mirror image, was much more independent. She would often wander off to explore on her own.

A grown-up Mabula taking a time-out.

And then there was Mnumzane, the young bull and son of the previous matriarch who had been demoted from crown prince to outsider after his mother's death. He was no longer part of the herd's inner circle and spent most of his time alone or at the edge of the group. This is the centuries-old elephant way. Herds are dominated by females. Once a male approaches puberty, he is evicted. But the trauma of young males being kicked out of their families can be heartrending. Luckily they usually meet up with other young, evicted males and form a loosely knit bachelor herd under the guidance of a wise old bull.

Unfortunately we didn't have a father figure for Mnumzane. He was going through the agony of losing his mother and sister at the same time as being cast out of the only family he knew and loved. Come feeding time, Nana and Frankie would roughly shoulder him away, and he only got scraps after everyone else had had their fill.

We saw he was losing weight, and so David made a point of feeding him separately. Mnumzane's gratitude was wrenching to watch. David started paying him special attention by slipping the bull extra alfalfa and fresh acacia branches every day.

Mnumzane's lowly status was confirmed one evening when we heard a series of prolonged, high-pitched squeals. Denied the use of the Land Rover by Wilma's web-building activities, we sprinted to the other side of the *boma* to see that Nana and Frankie had the youngster cornered and were shoving him onto the electric fence.

"Look at that," David said, panting as we ran up. "They're using him as a battering ram, trying to force him through to make an opening."

So they were. Mnumzane, caught between hot wires and a mountain of flesh and tusk, was screaming himself hoarse as electricity jolted through his young body. The more he screamed, the more they pushed.

Just as we were about to intervene—although I'm not quite sure how—they released him. The poor fellow bolted and ran around the *boma* at full speed, loudly trumpeting his indignation.

He calmed down and found a quiet spot as far away from the rest of herd as he could. There he stood and sulked, miserable to his core.

This incident showed conclusively that Nana and Frankie understood exactly how an electric fence worked. They knew that if they could bulldoze Mnumzane through the live wires, they could break free without getting shocked.

Despite this incident and to my intense relief, by now the dreaded dawn patrol had stopped. Nana no longer lined up her herd at the northern boundary, threatening a mass break-out. Against the odds, we seemed to have made some progress in the few weeks they had been with us.

But I didn't expect what happened next.

21

Soon after sunrise, I glanced up to see Nana and baby Mandla at the fence right in front of our little camp. This had never happened before.

As I stood, she lifted her trunk and looked straight at me. Her ears were down and she was calm. Instinctively, I decided to go to her.

I knew from hard experience that elephants prefer slow deliberate movements, so I ambled over, stopping to pluck a grass stem, pausing to inspect a tree stump, just generally taking my time. I needed to let Nana get used to me coming forward.

I stopped about three yards from the fence and gazed up at the gigantic form directly in front of me. Then I took one slow step forward. Then I took another and another, until I was two paces from the fence.

Nana did not move. Suddenly, I felt wrapped in a sense of contentment. I was standing mere inches away from this previously foul-tempered wild animal, who, until now, would have liked nothing better than to kill me. But I had never felt safer.

I remained in a bubble of well-being, completely captivated by the magnificent creature towering over me. I noticed for the first time her thick, wiry eyelashes, the thousands of wrinkles crisscrossing her skin, and her broken tusk. Her soft eyes pulled me in. Then, almost in slow motion, she gently reached out to me with her trunk. I watched, hypnotized, as if this were the most natural thing in the world.

David's voice echoed in the background. "Boss."

Then louder: "Boss! Boss, what are you doing?"

The urgency in his call broke the spell. Suddenly I realized that if Nana got hold of me it would be over. I would be yanked through the fence like a rag doll and stomped flat.

I was about to step back, but something made me hold my ground. There it was again, the strange feeling of peacefulness.

Once more, Nana stretched out her trunk. And then I got it. She wanted me to come closer. Without thinking, I moved toward the fence.

Time stood still as Nana's trunk snaked through the fence, carefully avoiding the electric strands, and reached my body. She gently touched me. I was surprised at the wetness of her trunk tip and how musky her smell was. After a few moments, I lifted my hand and felt the top of her colossal trunk, briefly stroking its bristly hairs.

It was over too soon. Nana slowly withdrew her trunk. She stood and looked at me for a few moments before she turned away. She returned to the herd, which had gathered about twenty yards behind her, watching our every move. Interestingly, Frankie stepped forward and greeted her, as if to welcome her back to the fold. If I didn't know better, I would have said she was giving Nana a "well done." I walked back to the camp.

"What was that about?" asked David.

I was silent for a while, absolutely awestruck. Then the words tumbled out: "I don't know. But what I do know is that it's time to let them out. We'll release them into the reserve early tomorrow."

The enormity of what we were about to do hit me. If I was wrong and the herd broke out of the main reserve, they would be killed. I started having second thoughts. But while doing the final fence patrol for the night, I noticed the elephants were more relaxed and calmer than I had ever seen them before. It was almost as if they anticipated something special was about to happen. That made me feel better.

At five a.m., a game guard radioed me from the energizer shed to say that power was off in the *boma*. David lifted the gate's hefty horizontal poles off their hinges.

I called out to Nana, who was standing at the fence about fifty yards away, and I deliberately walked in and out of the entrance a couple of times to show it was open. Then David and I went and stood on top of an anthill at a safe distance from the entrance to get a grandstand view.

For twenty minutes nothing happened. Eventually Nana ambled over to the gate and tested the space with her trunk for some invisible obstruction. Satisfied, she moved forward, herd in tow. Then she stopped halfway through the exit. For some reason she would go no farther.

Ten minutes later she was still standing there, motionless. I turned to David, "What's going on? Why doesn't she go out?"

"It must be the water in front of the gate," he said. "The trench we dug for the truck that delivered them is full of rain, and she doesn't like it. I think she won't go through because it's too deep for Mandla."

Then, for the first time, we witnessed a graphic demonstration of Nana's Herculean strength.

On either side of the gate stood two eight-foot-high, eight-inch-wide eucalyptus poles sunk thirty inches into concrete. Nana inspected these with her trunk, then put her head down and gave a push. The shafts buckled as the concrete foundations popped out of the ground like corks.

David and I stared at each other, stunned. "We couldn't even have done that with the tractor," I said. "And to think that yesterday I was letting her touch me!"

The way around the trench was now clear, and Nana wasted no more time. She hurried the herd down a game path directly to the river. We watched the thick summer bush swallow them up.

I hoped we had done the right thing.

22

I dropped off David at the lodge, then drove to the Ovambo guards' cottage to give them an update.

I was about hundred yards away when Ndonga came sprinting up, waving his arms. "Quick, Mr. Anthony. Turn off the motor and keep quiet," he whispered. "There's a leopard about forty yards ahead, just to the right."

I killed the engine and squinted into the bush. The thicket was certainly large enough to hide a leopard. But leopards are mostly nocturnal animals. It would be highly unusual to see one at midday.

Then, out of the corner of my eye, I spotted one of the Ovambos come out from behind the house and nod at Ndonga. He was wiping his hands with a rag, which he quickly stuffed into his pocket when he saw me looking at him.

Ndonga, who had been crouching near the car, stood up and said the Land Rover must have scared it off.

"We've let the herd out," I told him. "Put all of your guards on patrol to track them. Also, check the fences. Make sure the power stays up permanently. And double-check that there are no trees anywhere even remotely close by the wires. I don't want the elephants shorting them again."

"I've already done that," Ndonga replied. "All trees near the fence have been chopped."

The last time I had heard that was just before the herd had escaped from the *boma*. I didn't want to risk it again.

I drove off and headed home. The bush around me was full, bright, and thick. Unfortunately, as beautiful as it looked, the thick foliage would make the elephants more difficult to track. We needed to know exactly where they were at all times in case they attempted another breakout.

As I walked through the door, Françoise told me that Ngwenya, my security *induna*, or foreman, wanted to see me.

He was sitting on a tree stump outside of the rangers' quarters. He obviously didn't want to be seen approaching me. So, I walked over to him.

"*Sawubona*, Ngwenya." *I see you.*

"*Yebo*, Mkhulu."

We spoke for a bit about the unusually wet weather and the elephants. Then he said, "Mkhulu, we all know strange things are happening."

"Such as what?"

"Such as the shooting of game on Thula Thula."

I stiffened. I had been so absorbed in the elephants that I had put the poaching problem on a back burner.

"Now I am also hearing strange stories," Ngwenya continued. "The strangest of all is that people are saying that Ndonga is the man doing the shooting and killing our animals."

"What?" The blood drained from my face. "What makes you say such a serious thing?"

Ngwenya shook his head, as if he too couldn't believe it. "Ndonga shoots the buck, but the skinning is done by the other Ovambos and by Phineas, the gate guard. Then sometimes a truck with no lights comes and fetches it. Or sometimes Ndonga takes the meat to town."

"How do you know this?"

"It is what the people here are saying. Also, I am told the other Ovambos are unhappy. They complain in the village that they are doing all the hard work and Ndonga gives them no money. He gives them only meat. Not even good meat. They get maybe the head and shins. That's all."

"How long has this been going on?"

Ngwenya shrugged. "Since the day you came. But I have only found this out now. That is why I have come to you."

"Thanks, Ngwenya. Good work."

"These are dangerous times." He eased himself off the stump. "The Ovambos must not know I have spoken to you. *Sale gahle*, Mkhulu." *Stay well.*

"*Hamba gahle*, Ngwenya." *Go well.*

I sat there, stunned. This was a horrific accusation, not just because the poachers had killed so many animals. That was bad enough. But if what Ngwenya said was true, then my own employees were guilty of poaching my animals with my own rifles.

Just then, David came over and told me that the electrician had arrived. We wanted him to thoroughly check the fence's electricity now that the elephants had been freed from the *boma*. As we got into the Land Rover, the radio crackled into life. It was Ndonga. I tensed with anger. Even though my head guard may be innocent and I had to give him the benefit of the doubt, Ngwenya's story deeply upset me.

"We've found the elephants on the northern boundary."

"Excellent," I replied, fighting to keep the fury out of my voice. "Keep an eye on them and wait for us."

It made sense that the herd had emerged at the far border, but it was chilling news. That was in the direction of their previous home. Were they still determined to break out?

23

As Ndonga had said, gangs of workers had chopped down all trees within felling distance of the wires. Narrow vehicle tracks had been hacked out to make a rough road for anti-poaching patrols and maintenance checks along the boundary. So it was relatively simple to keep the animals in sight as we followed from a distance.

Nana was moving along the fence line. She had placed the tip of her trunk just below the top electric strand to sense the pulse of the surging current. With her clan following her, she had walked almost the entire reserve's perimeter, about twenty miles. She was using her "natural volt meter" to see if any section of the fence did not have power.

This had taken the animals most of the day. I was relieved to see that, apart from checking for breaks in the power, Nana did not try to touch the fence. She wasn't going to take the pain and smash through it.

But as the herd was completing its tour, we saw a lone, large acacia tree right next to the wires. Ndonga's clearing gang had somehow missed it, and it stood out as stark as a monument.

David and I knew what was going to happen next.

Sure enough, Nana and Frankie stopped, saw the tree, and loped over for a closer inspection.

"No, Nana, no!" I shouted as they positioned themselves on either side of the acacia and started shouldering it, testing its resistance. There was no doubt they were going to shove it down. If we were going to prevent a breakout, we needed to get closer. I was glad a gate was nearby. We sped out of the reserve and onto a road on the opposite side of the fence.

The tree creaked wildly on its roots, and Nana gave it a mighty heave. *Crack!* The tree trunk splintered down onto the fence. The poles collapsed, and the current was short circuited. Without thinking about the potential danger, I rushed up and snatched at the wires to see if they were still live. As I feared, the fence was dead.

We had a real problem.

"No, Nana, don't do it!" I yelled. There was only a tangle of dead wires and flattened poles between us. My voice was raspy with desperation: "Don't do it!"

Fortunately the clicking and snapping of the wires as they shorted out had spooked her. She took a hasty step backward. But for how long?

We were lucky to have the electrician there. While I pleaded with the agitated animals, he and David got to work. With Nana, Frankie, and the youngsters barely ten yards away, the two men calmly untangled the bird's nest of wires, chopped the tree free, reconnected the cable, straightened the poles, and got the power going again.

All the while, I continued speaking directly to Nana. I kept using her name and repeated again and again that this was her home.

For at least ten minutes, Nana held eye contact with me as I talked.

Suddenly, as if baffled by all the fuss, she turned and went back into the bush. The others followed, and we exhaled with relief.

It was only then that I realized I hadn't even considered picking up a rifle in case everything went wrong. My relationship with the herd had certainly deepened.

I realized something else. As the tree came down—to a man—the Ovambos had bolted like startled rabbits. This was strange, I thought. Were they actually afraid of elephants? That was not what I would have expected from such experienced men of the bush.

Then it dawned on me. It was as if I were seeing clearly for the first time. These men were not game rangers at all. They were soldiers who could shoot straight, but they knew precious little about conservation. I had always wondered why the Ovambos, who were supposed to be the best animal trackers, had led us the wrong way during the herd's original breakout. Now I knew.

It had become as obvious as the sun beating down on us. The guards were the poachers, exactly as Ngwenya had said. They were the ones who had been shooting all the bucks. And the last thing they wanted was a herd of wild elephants on Thula Thula.

Having no experience with elephants, let alone this

unpredictable herd, they realized that with angry jumbos around their poaching racket would be ruined. The reason was simple: Most poaching is done in the dark, and one would have to be brave, or monumentally foolish, to trample around in the bush at night with this temperamental herd on the loose. It would be suicide. They needed to engineer another elephant escape so their poaching business could continue.

Even though I had no hard evidence, the jigsaw pieces started fitting together. I suddenly remembered that Bheki had told me that a "gun had spoken" at the *boma* on the night the elephants first escaped. Could someone have deliberately fired those shots to panic the herd and cause a frenzied stampede?

Now I also understood why the fence wires had initially been strung on the wrong side of the *boma* poles. And, of course, no leopard had been at the cottage earlier this morning. I would bet anything that they had been butchering illegally slaughtered animals, and my unexpected arrival had almost caught them red-handed. Ndonga had to distract me while they hurried to hide the evidence. That's why the game guard had come out from the back of the house wiping off his hands. They had been covered with blood.

And what about the lone tree that had been left standing right at the fence? That was probably the most obvious clue of all. It was far too coincidental not to have been deliberate.

I had been set up.

Not only had we been betrayed, but more important, the elephants were now in danger.

24

As we drove off, I told David everything. He was just as furious as I was. I said we needed to put our best rangers alongside the Ovambos twenty-four hours a day, so the rangers could watch every move they made. This would prevent the Ovambos from being able to shoot any more animals. It would also buy us some time to gather hard evidence.

The next morning we were out early to see what the elephants were doing. We found them grazing in the middle of the reserve, about as far from the fence as you could get. Mnumzane was a hundred yards or so from the main group, stripping leaves from a small acacia. We eased forward until we were close enough to see the herd clearly, and I did a head count. Seven. They were all there, engulfed by long grass and succulent trees, stuffing their mouths like kids at a birthday party.

The tranquility of this scene made everything worthwhile. After all the stress, drama, danger, and frustration, this hugely aggressive herd at last seemed serene in their new home. At least for the moment.

"They're exploring and they like what they see," said

David. "This must be better than anything they've known before."

I nodded. Maybe, just maybe, our gamble in letting them out of the *boma* early had paid off.

The herd enjoying a peaceful moment in the grass.

25

One morning I decided to spend some time with the elephants to make sure that Nana and her herd were indeed settling in.

After about an hour's drive I found them shading themselves under a sprawling, giant fig tree right next to the river. Although it was still early, it was already almost one hundred degrees. I stopped the Land Rover, crept forward, and settled down under a leafy marula tree about fifty yards downwind of them. They stood motionless, except for gently flapping their ears to cool themselves as best they could.

Mnumzane was about twenty yards closer to me than the rest of the herd was. He sensed my presence and moved slightly nearer. He continued grazing but glanced up every now and again to watch me. It seemed he preferred my company to that of the other elephants. He made no effort to raise an alarm to them that I was there.

Mnumzane was superb. He was well proportioned and had strong tusks. He would soon grow into a great bull, lord of all he surveyed. At the moment, however, he was just a confused and lost teenager, still aching from the death of his mother.

In the background, Nana found a succulent young paper-bark acacia tree and decided it was ideal for a family lunch. She pushed gently, testing the tree's strength. Then she adjusted her angle, put her head down, and with a push-relax-push motion worked up massive momentum. The tree rocked violently, and as it swayed at the very end of its tether, she gave it a final shove, and it came splintering down. The rest of the herd ambled across to join in the feast.

The sound of the tree crashing stilled the bush for a few moments, and I noticed a nearby family of nyalas prick up their ears. The bull scented the air, knowing instinctively what had happened. Once the elephants moved off, the nyalas would be able to gorge on the felled acacia's juicy top leaves that they would've never been able to reach otherwise. In fact, during dry winters when grazing is poor, herds of antelopes often shadow elephants for days waiting for the matriarch to bulldoze a tree.

The noise had also alarmed a leguaan, a large African monitor lizard, that had been raiding birds' nests up in a red-flowered weeping *boerbeen* tree overhanging the river. Startled, the four-foot-long, black-gray reptile sprang off a high branch, twisted through the air, and belly-flopped into the river.

At my feet, my dog, Max, heard the splash. He must have thought it was a snake. He always had a hard time resisting the urge to chase and attack snakes. Max was off like a shot into the reeds before I could grab him. Crocodiles lived in that river and splashing about in it was suicidal enough for large animals, let alone a dog. When Max came out and shook his dripping torso like a sprinkler, I sternly reprimanded him.

None of this bothered the elephants. Nana, Nandi, and Mandla stood on one side of the fallen tree. Frankie, Marula, and Mabula stood on the other. They all methodically converted leaves and bark into edible mulch, using the most powerful molars in the animal kingdom. I couldn't help but notice that the elephants often instinctively bunched into two groups. Although they had become one family, each group was the remnant of a much larger herd that had been cruelly whittled down by sales and executions.

The wind shifted, and I knew the elephants could now smell me in their presence. I needed to move fast in case they began to charge toward me. As I stood, I saw the tip of Nana's trunk suddenly angle and swivel toward me, snatching a trace of my scent. She stood back and lifted her trunk to verify the odor. Then she turned to face in my direction.

I collected my binoculars and water bottle and climbed into the Land Rover with Max just as Nana started to advance toward me. The rest of the herd was behind her. I had plenty of time to drive off, but I was intrigued that she was actually heading my way. Normally, she would have hurriedly herded her family in the opposite direction.

I moved the Land Rover into a good getaway position, steeled my nerves, and waited. At the last moment, mere yards away, Nana changed direction ever so slightly and walked past the vehicle. She was followed by her family. Each one turned to stare at me as they passed. Frankie, bringing up the rear, splayed her ears and gave an aggressive shake of her head toward me.

Then suddenly Frankie swung off the back of the line, trumpeted harshly, and started coming at me, fast as a truck— her ears flared, and her trunk raised high. I knew instinctively that this was a mock charge. The worst thing I could do was drive off, because this could encourage her, and perhaps spark a serious, real charge. I braced myself as she pulled up just yards away in a whirlwind of flapping ears, dust, and rage. After she tossed her head in anger once or twice, she stomped back to the herd with her tail angrily erect.

I stared after her, transfixed. Even though I had seen it many times, a charging elephant is one of the most awesome sights in the world. Once I regained my ability to think, I realized that I'd have to be careful with Frankie. She was still ill-tempered and too eager to vent her fury. Nana was the matriarch, but Frankie was far more dangerous.

26

I followed the herd for a bit, thorns scratching the Land Rover's paintwork, until the bush became too wild. Then I turned and headed home.

I had just gulped down a pint of ice-cold water when the phone rang. It was the wildlife dealer again, urging me to sell him the herd. This time, before I got off the phone, I got his company's name. Then I called Marion at EMOA to ask about the dealer.

"They are registered wildlife dealers, perfectly legitimate," she told me. "But I've heard they had already pre-sold your animals to a Chinese zoo. That's why I was in such a hurry to get them to you. They're pretty upset with me and are now trying to get the animals back to fulfill their contract. If you sell them to him, your elephants' lives will be a misery. There are few animal-rights laws in China, so anything could happen. And even worse, the zoo wants only the babies, so the two adults will probably be shot. Please don't deal with them."

"Well, you can relax," I said, relieved to finally hear the truth. "My elephants are going nowhere."

I phoned the dealer and told him politely never to contact me again.

He was floored. He then hesitated for a bit, but then he said, "Listen, don't tell my boss I told you this, but the previous matriarch, the one they shot, wasn't so bad. I reckon she was just trying to get the herd to better water and grazing. That's why she kept busting the fences. She was just doing her job."

I put the phone down as that revelation slowly sunk in. The old matriarch had been doing her duty to her family—and she had paid for it with her life. They had even shot her baby daughter. My anger flared. No wonder this herd was traumatized.

27

In the meantime, I decided to confront Phineas, the gate guard, who was one of the poachers. I was gambling that, if faced with being turned over to the police, he would decide to side with us and become our key witness. I was right.

Phineas's head slumped to his chest, and without warning, he began to sob. No doubt his conscience had been bothering him. He confessed, apologized, and then gave me the full details of the poaching ring. He told me exactly what species and how many animals they had shot. He gave me the dates and times of the attacks, too. I was astounded by the scale of the operation. The Ovambos had slaughtered at least a hundred animals, which translates into several tons of meat and thousands of dollars.

We spent the rest of the day interviewing other staff fingered by Phineas, collecting facts, and taking more statements. We definitely had a case, but I decided to wait and see what other stories would emerge.

My rangers moved into quarters next to the Ovambos, and David became Ndonga's "new best friend." I also started calling Ndonga over the radio at all hours, asking where the

Ovambos were. I held meetings in the bush and also made surprise visits to their house. They were never alone and so had no opportunity to poach.

Unable to hunt due to our constant surveillance, the Ovambos began to slip out to the village at night to drink at the local shebeen, an illegal tavern. The more they drank, the more they talked. They began to brag openly about their poaching exploits. We, of course, always had an informer there, and slowly we were able to complete our case.

We drove into Empangeni to meet with two senior policemen. We told them the full story and handed over all the sworn statements. We were told we had an open-and-shut case.

At five p.m. on the dot, two police vans arrived at the reserve. David and I led them to the Ovambos' cottage. We were too late. All the Ovambos' personal possessions were gone. They must have seen us coming and run off into the bush. There was no way we would catch them before dark.

The police said they would put a general alert out for the fleeing guards. That was all we could do for the moment.

Back at the house I filled Françoise in, and we strolled outside, where we watched the bloodred sun ease itself down beyond the sweeping hills. The reserve looked tranquil. Perhaps I was imagining it, but with the guards gone, it felt as if the whole mood of the reserve had changed. It was as if some particularly evil force had been purged.

28

After that, it felt like Thula Thula was, at last, finding its footing.

The elephants weren't trying to be serial escapers, and the poaching problem was largely solved. I knew we would never entirely stamp out poaching. In Africa, a few people shooting an impala or a duiker for the cooking pot is going to happen no matter what you do.

For the first time since we had purchased Thula Thula, I could concentrate on our core mission: running an African game reserve.

It is a tough, rewarding life. Each day starts at dawn. Not only are there no weekends, but if you are not careful you can quickly lose track of the days of the week. Fences have to be checked and fixed daily. Roads and tracks must be repaired and brought back from bush encroachment or you will lose them forever. Then there are game counts, grass-land assessments, dam inspections and repairs, fire-break maintenance, and anti-poaching patrols. In addition, you need to maintain good relations with neighboring groups, and do a hundred or so other important things. But it is a good, clean life with just enough danger and adventure to keep you on your toes.

© SUKIDHANDRA

Me with Vusi (left), Bheki (rear), and Ngwenya (right).

I spent as much time as I could near the elephant herd. They had only been out of the *boma* for three weeks, but they were noticeably gaining weight because they were stuffing themselves on a variety of plant delicacies.

I always stayed a comfortable distance away from them and tried to blend in as much as possible. In this way I learned a lot about them, including where their favorite watering holes were and what they liked to eat.

Sometimes things didn't go as planned. Once, when I thought the herd was some distance away, I got out of the Land Rover to make a call on my brand-new cell phone. Something made me look over my shoulder. To my horror, Frankie was about twenty yards behind me. And behind her was the rest of the herd.

I sprinted to the Land Rover, yanked open the door, and leapt inside. In my haste, I dropped my fancy new phone, and the elephants were now milling around near it. I had no option but to wait until they moved off before I could get it back.

Then it rang. The ringtone pierced the wilderness like a whistle blast. The elephants stopped and, almost in unison, moved over to the source of the alien noise. Frankie got there first and snaked her trunk over the piece of plastic, trying to figure out what it was. The others joined in, and I watched this bizarre spectacle of seven elephants swinging their trunks over a chirruping cell phone in the middle of the bush.

Finally Frankie decided she had had enough. She lifted her mighty foot above the phone and brought it down with a thud. The ringing stopped.

The herd moved off, ambling along in their own sweet time. When they were finally out of sight, I went to get the phone. It was embedded an inch into the ground. I had to pry it loose. The clear plastic section of the casing was shattered.

As an experiment I punched in a number. It went through, and I heard the line ring. Amazingly the phone still worked.

29

With the Ovambo guards gone, a lot of other animals suddenly reappeared. Wherever I went, I saw kudus, nyalas, herds of wildebeests and impalas, and a host of smaller game scurrying about, seemingly without a care in the world. Before I bought the land, hunters had taken a shot at any creature that moved. Then during my first year, the poachers had muscled in. They had blinded antelope with megawatt spotlights and shot at them from vehicles both at night and during the day. No wonder the animals had been so skittish whenever a Land Rover drove past. A car engine had been enough to set the entire reserve into panic mode—with good reason, I now realized.

Up to this point, the only time I really had occasion to appreciate Thula Thula's wildlife had been when David and I camped outside the *boma*. No longer. Almost overnight, a major transformation occurred. Hyenas became bolder in the evenings, and we even got glimpses of leopards, lynxes, and servals. The more the creatures lost their fear, the more of them we saw. I was astonished that, somehow, the animals knew the poachers were gone.

With great joy, we discovered we still had healthy populations of almost all the local animals despite the poaching. The whole reserve was now truly energized—as we were along with it.

Rangers on a bush walk—a favorite with visitors.

One morning, when I went to track the elephant herd, Françoise joined me on the quad bike, a four-wheeled all-terrain motorbike. With her arms tight around my waist, we rode through a shallow section of the Nseleni River to a high lookout point.

We spotted the elephants briefly in thick bush that bordered the river below, close to where we had just come through. We must have missed them only by about fifty yards. It worried me that I hadn't detected them sooner, especially with Françoise riding with me. I had a feeling of unease I was unable to shake; normally I was able to sense when the elephants were around.

"There they are again." I pointed, and we watched the elephants lope single file into view about a mile away.

"They're moving off," I said. "Let's give them a bit of time to cross the river, and then we can go after them."

About ten minutes later we rode back down the hill, and I slowly eased the bike down into the lazily flowing river. Once we made it to the other side, we shot to the top of the riverbank.

Suddenly I became aware of huge gray shapes all around us. We had ridden right into the middle of the herd! The elephants had stopped to graze right at the exit of the river crossing. This was something I had not anticipated; I had thought they were on the move.

Shock shuddered through my body. I felt minuscule, puny, and unprotected on a tiny bike surrounded by edgy, five-ton mammals. Even worse, I had Françoise with me. My throat tightened and my mind raced. How do I get us out of this?

Especially troublesome was that we had unintentionally cut off Marula and Mabula from their mother, Frankie. The two young elephants were behind us, and they panicked and started squealing loudly. If one thing could aggravate our already terrible predicament even more, it was getting between an aggressive female elephant and her frightened young.

We were in trouble. Deep trouble.

30

Nana was a few yards away, on our right. She took two menacing steps forward with her trunk held high, and then stopped and backed off. That was terrifying enough, but the real problem was behind her. Frankie.

I frantically tried to turn the bike so we could bolt away. But the riverbank was too steep, and the bike's turning circle was too wide. We were trapped.

Trying to sound as unconcerned as possible, I said to Françoise, surprised that my voice was still steady, "I think we have a problem." I was absolutely horrified that I had placed her in such danger.

By now Frankie was furiously reversing out of a thicket, trying to swivel and charge us. I handed my pistol to Françoise to protect herself if anything happened to me. Basically, it was a peashooter as far as an elephant was concerned, but as a last resort, a shot might distract Frankie.

I then stood up on the bike to face Frankie, who was now coming directly at us—fast, furious, and deadly. I silently pleaded that this be a mock charge and desperately looked for signs that she just wanted to scare us away from her young.

The key indication of this would be if her ears flapped out. But no. With mounting horror, I watched Frankie fold her ears back and roll up her trunk to take full impact when she hit us.

That rolled trunk meant she was going all the way. This was for real, and with that awful realization my senses heightened. I heard someone hammering in the far-off village as if it were next door, while high above me I watched an eagle soar. I marveled at its graceful flight, like I had nothing better to do.

On Frankie hurtled, her huge frame blotting out all else. I lifted my hands as high above my head as I could and I started to yell at her. I screamed at the monstrous sight in a last-ditch attempt to pierce through her mist of rage.

Just as I thought we were goners, Frankie's ears suddenly cracked out. She broke off and unrolled her trunk. Her massive momentum had hurled her right up to the bike, though. She towered directly above us, glaring angrily down at us through her tiny eyes. I involuntarily sat down on the bike and looked up at the crinkled underside of Frankie's throat in petrified wonder. She shook her huge head in frustration and showered us in thick red dust from a recent sand bath. Then she backed off a few paces.

Marula and Mabula scampered past her. After making another two or three terrifyingly threatening gestures at us, Frankie turned and followed her son and daughter into the bush.

I eased down off the bike's saddle and turned to Françoise.

Her eyes were tightly closed. I gently whispered that it was over. The two of us sat still, too stunned to do or say anything.

Eventually, I found the energy to start the bike and pulled off in the opposite direction from the herd. We drove through the bush, which now seemed still, as if the birds and trees themselves knew what had happened.

Back home I told the astonished staff about our encounter. "I can't believe you're still alive," said David, whistling through his teeth. "She must have made a conscious decision not to kill you. Why do you think she did that?"

A good question. Elephants rarely break off once they're at full steam. I still couldn't believe that Frankie had actually halted at the last minute. Why had she changed gears from a real, lethal attack to a mock charge? It was virtually unheard of.

The next day I got on the bike and drove back to the river crossing where we had so nearly lost our lives to try to figure it out. But try as I might, the crucial moments of the charge were a total blank. It was as if my mind couldn't grapple with the horror.

So I retraced our route. I drove through the same river crossing several times and slowly started to flesh out the details. I remembered I had been standing on the bike and screaming as she charged. But what was I yelling? My mind was still a void.

Then in an instant, it came flooding back. I had been screaming, "Stop, stop, it's me, it's me!"

That was all. It sounds rather ridiculous and lame to shout "It's me" at a charging elephant who happens to be the most aggressive female in a herd and who is protecting her panicked babies. Yet it had stopped her. I knew then that she had somehow recognized me from the *boma*. I believed—and still do—that she had spared our lives because she had witnessed her matriarch's interaction with me the day before I let them out.

31

We were having endless problems with the fence. Everything affected it. Too much rain drowned the current. Too little rain affected the transmission of electricity. Lightning struck the fence often, and that cut the voltage. Hyenas, bushpigs, and warthogs constantly dug holes beneath it, shorting the circuit. Sometimes the power seemed to go down just because it felt like it. It certainly didn't make keeping the elephants inside the reserve any easier.

Not that they were trying to escape. But what if Nana was walking near the boundary and sensed there was no power? What would happen? Because we did not know the answer to that, we had daily dawn-and-dusk inspections along the entire twenty-mile perimeter of the reserve. And we never went to bed unless the fence was fully operational.

Right now, though, not only was the power down, but the Land Rover also wouldn't start, and it was getting dark.

"No problem," said David. "I'll take the tractor."

I looked across at Gunda Gunda, the name of our twenty-year-old tractor. She was reliable all right and would do the job, but she had no headlights, and a twenty-mile drive in the bush in the dark can be tough. It's so black you can't see anything—and I mean anything. Unless you can navigate by the stars (provided there is no cloud cover), you'll be lost within minutes. And don't forget that every nocturnal creature out there can see everything—including you—with absolute clarity.

Despite my reservations, David jumped up on Gunda Gunda and set off. After he left, I realized he had forgotten his radio.

I was trying to spot David's flashlight blinking on the far boundary when I heard a low moan that rose into a rasping roar. My blood chilled. Max also froze and stared out into the dark, alert.

I heard it again. It was a male lion. We had no lions on the reserve; this one must have broken in.

Then to make things worse, another lion roared in response. It was a bloodcurdling growl that bounced off the cliffs. That meant there were at least *two* lions on the reserve. And of all places, the roars were coming from exactly where David was driving along without headlights. They must have come in through an opening in the fence while the power was down.

Out in the dark, every creature in the reserve had surely heard the lions' roars, which were death itself calling.

I imagined Nana standing frozen, ears flared, trunk up, smelling the air to work out where the call came from and worrying about the youngsters in the herd. Her behavior would now change, as would everything else on the reserve.

It sometimes happened that lions broke out of the Umfolozi

game reserve. They raided cattle and generally struck fear in the villages. Lions on the loose totally control the country-side. They're difficult to corner, and they find cattle and other livestock exceptionally easy prey. If the lions become too much of a problem, they are usually hunted down and killed by rangers.

I love lions, but I wished this pair had gone somewhere else. And I was very concerned about David. While he was on the tractor with its noise and greasy fumes, he was relatively safe. But he was looking for an electrical fault, and to find it he would have to get off the vehicle and walk along the fence, sometimes for long distances. I knew he was carrying a small flashlight, but he had no rifle with him. Walking unarmed in the bush at night with lions in the immediate vicinity is crazy stuff. I was hoping against hope that he had also heard the calls. But Gunda Gunda is pretty noisy, and I couldn't be sure.

We had to go find him. I called Bheki at the rangers' house and told him to get my rifle and to bring plenty of bul-lets. I wasn't looking forward to the march in the dark, but there was a rough dirt track running along the outside of the fence for much of the way. We should be safe there, since the big cats were inside the reserve.

Then we heard that spine-chilling roar again. It was close, perhaps only a mile or two away. By now I was acutely alarmed. The lions must have smelled the tractor. Had they also detected the human driver? And just how hungry were they? They may not have eaten for several days.

The second lion roared in reply to the first lion. The sound was even closer this time.

Gripping our rifles tight, Bheki and I broke into a jog. Well, we went as fast as you can go in the darkness. Even with flashlights, it is always difficult out in the bush at night. We paid no attention to our numerous trips and falls over rocks and bush roots. Our only goal was to get to David before the lions did.

About two miles later, we saw a dim flickering light, and to our intense joy we saw that it was David. He was at a gap in the fence. Gunda Gunda chugged away close by.

I was about to yell a warning, but he beat me to it.

"Lion! Big ones!" he shouted, then pointed to the hole. "They came in there. I left the tractor running to keep them away. Their spoor is all over the place."

Relief washed over me. This guy was indestructible. "Leave the tractor here for the night and walk back with us on the outside path."

We closed the hole the lions had dug under the fence and pushed up the wires. This is what had shorted the electricity. We got the power back up, which effectively trapped the lions in the reserve. Then we walked home. The next day promised to be interesting.

32

Etiquette in the bush dictates that telephone calls are allowable only after dawn. The sun was barely up when I had the Parks Board section ranger on the line.

"Have you lost a couple of lions?" I asked.

"Yes," he replied. "Two got out the day before yesterday and have been causing chaos around a couple of villages. They're on the move, going your way actually. Have you seen them?"

"They're both in Thula," I replied. "Do you want to come and get them?"

"We're on our way."

All the reserve staff were told to be extra cautious, and the work teams were sent home. None of our employees had experience with lions, so we weren't taking any chances.

While we were waiting for the Parks Board to arrive, I went out to find the herd. I picked up their tracks and shortly afterward found fresh elephant dung within yards of fresh lion scat. The herd had crossed paths with the big cats, but there was no real risk. An elephant herd is far too challenging for lions, however hungry they might be. That is, provided the youngsters didn't wander off.

I couldn't find the herd, so I went back to the house. Standing on the front lawn staring out into the bush, I remembered a harrowing incident the previous year when a hunting lioness charged Craig Reed, the senior ranger at Umfolozi. He was out on horseback with his five-months' pregnant wife, Andrea, when the giant cat suddenly charged at them. Craig's horse was spooked and bolted, but the lioness had already targeted Andrea and chased after her.

An expert rider, Andrea galloped through the bush at full speed. Scenting the danger, the horse needed no encouragement and was in full flight when Andrea's foot slipped out of the stirrup and she started to slide off the saddle.

As she fell, she somehow managed to grab hold of the stirrup and was dragged through the bush as the horse galloped on with the lioness in hot pursuit. Andrea watched, horrified, as the lioness got closer and closer until it was at her feet, and then, resigned to her fate, she let go. Amazingly the lioness jumped right over Andrea's sprawling body and got her claws into the horse.

By now Craig had managed to turn his horse. He rode up and frantically fired shots into the air to scare off the lioness. Thankfully Andrea, although badly bruised and shaken, was okay. She gave birth to a fine baby boy four months later.

The moral of the story is to always treat these magnificent creatures with absolute respect. I pondered this over a hurried breakfast and then met up with Bheki and his men to follow the spoor from the hole where the big cats had come in.

After a few hours, the trail disappeared. We noticed that there weren't any vultures circling above. This meant that the lions hadn't made a kill during the night. If they had, the vultures would be circling over the remains. That would have given us a general direction to head in.

When the Parks Board arrived, we searched the reserve for two days. We kept picking up and losing the trail. Finally, a fence check revealed a big hole under the wire. They were gone. We later heard that they had returned to Umfolozi.

33

The elephant is the largest land mammal on earth. The southern white rhino is the second largest. It can easily weigh three tons and is targeted by poachers for its horns. We had just had three southern white rhinos delivered to the reserve. One female, still dopey from the sedatives, had groggily wandered away from the other two. This posed a big problem. The elephants were close by, and she was, unknowingly, ambling directly toward them. We had to cut her off.

Trying to dissuade a mountain of muscle and horn still hungover from travel tranquilizers from going in her chosen direction was not something I wanted to do. I radioed David to grab some large sacks of horse feed and meet me with the Land Rover at the south end of the airstrip. While I waited for him, I watched the beautiful creature, not fifteen yards away, walk unsteadily. Her short dumpy legs could usually propel her into an unbelievably fast charge in no time. Clad in a suit of armor that could withstand almost anything except a bullet, she tottered along, completely unaware of my presence. She had a magnificent forty-inch horn at the tip of her head.

I also kept a cautious eye on the elephant herd browsing

upwind. I heard a soft sound behind me and turned to see Mnumzane coming along the airstrip downwind, testing the air.

Of all the bad luck! He must have caught either my or the rhino's scent. He slowly started to walk in our direction.

David arrived, pulled up next to me, and jumped out, leaving the motor idling.

"Somehow we have to keep Mnumzane and the herd away from her," I said, pointing to the dazed rhino. "They're too close. I really don't like this at all."

"The horse feed should delay him for a while," he replied.

"Yeah, but the smell might also bring the other elephants over. We're going to have to shield the rhino with the Land Rover, put ourselves between her and any elephant that gets too curious. But first let's try and get Mnumzane out of the way."

David jumped into the back of the Landy and opened a large sack of horse pellets. He placed the open bag at the tailgate and crouched down next to it. "I hope they like this stuff."

"We'll soon find out," I said, getting behind the wheel and driving slowly toward Mnumzane.

This was a deadly serious business. Usually elephants will bother rhinos only if they don't get out of their way, which rhinos will do. However, our latest addition was still shaking off the effects of sedatives. She might stumble into Mnumzane or the herd. Just about anything could happen.

What we planned to do was divert Mnumzane's attention away from the groggy rhino first by giving him a taste of the protein-rich pellets. Then we would lay a food trail to entice him as far away as possible. David would be completely exposed on the open back of the pickup as he poured the feed out to an excited elephant following just yards behind. Mnumzane was only a teenager, but he still weighed about three and a half tons. It was dangerous work.

I cut across in front of Mnumzane, then reversed back to where he stood confused and a little grumpy about this noisy intrusion in his space. David chucked out some feed, and I drove off a short distance. To our dismay, he ignored the offering and resumed his meander up the airstrip toward the rhino.

"Reverse again!" shouted David, holding the bag, ready to pour. "But this time get much closer.

"Closer, closer!" David called as I gingerly edged the vehicle backward toward the young bull.

Suddenly, not liking what was going on, Mnumzane lifted his head aggressively and turned sharply toward us, his ears spread wide.

"Just a little bit more . . . ," said David, ignoring the elephant's blatant warning. When I thought we were too close, he quickly tipped the bag, and I slammed the vehicle into first, easing forward. As we went, David laid a long line of feed that led away from the rhino.

Mnumzane watched us go. He relaxed his flared ears and unfurled his trunk to smell the pile of pellets on the ground. He snuffled some into his mouth, and seconds later he was piling it in like a glutton. The ploy had worked.

"That will keep him busy, and we've plenty more chow if

the others come across," said David as he hopped off the back and got into the passenger seat, shoving Max between us.

At the mention of the other elephants, I looked to where they were grazing about forty yards away. As I did so, Nana's trunk suddenly snaked up. An elephant has such a superb sense of smell that, even upwind, she can pick up minute bits of odor that are swirling ever so slightly in the air.

With the herd following, she started moving toward us, checking the air continuously, sniffing for the source of the scent. We now had the herd coming in on one side of the poor rhino and Mnumzane on the other. Even worse, they weren't advancing in single file, which would have been much more manageable. Nana was in the center with Frankie, Frankie's daughter and son were on the left, and Nana's son and daughter were on the right.

Straight in front of them, still hidden in the bush, was the woozy rhino. To my dismay, she had begun to settle down for a rest, which made her even more vulnerable to the approaching elephants.

David leapt onto the back of the Land Rover again and this time cut open two bags and got ready to pour a trail while I reversed in.

The herd picked up the scent and cautiously came toward us, while David scooped pellets out as fast as possible. Frankie's youngsters, Mabula and Marula, stopped and started sniffing at the strange fare. The rest, led by Nana and Frankie, continued on, slowly following the trail left behind the Land Rover.

Then, of all things, the Land Rover stalled and I couldn't

restart it. Thankfully the cabin's rear window had long since lost its glass. With Nana almost on top of him, David somehow squeezed his large body through the tiny gap and in a tangle of limbs dived onto Max in the passenger seat.

Then the elephants were upon us. We were surrounded.

Fortunately, it was the feed the elephants were after. The two adults yanked the remaining bags off the back and tried standing on them to smash them open. Frankie, frustrated in her attempts to open one bag, grabbed it by the corner with her trunk and flicked it high into the air—luckily in the opposite direction from the now-sleeping rhino. It sailed above our heads for at least thirty yards and landed with a thud, its contents scattering. Given that the bag weighed 120 pounds and she had grasped it only with the tip of her trunk, the height and distance of the throw were truly remarkable.

The elephants loped off after the broken bag, and while they were busy gorging themselves, we were able to sneak out to fix the Land Rover. It was a disconnected fuel line, and we restarted the vehicle pretty quickly. Now knowing that they loved horse feed, I radioed for more, and we laid tasty trails of food to lead the herd far away from the rhino.

34

We weren't so lucky, though, with Mnumzane. He had unfinished business with the rhino and soon lost interest in the scraps of feed on the ground. He walked back toward where she lay.

There was nothing left to do but get between them and keep him away as best we could. My heart jumped at the thought, for even at his age he could easily toss our vehicle over if he wanted to. Bull elephants don't like to be forced to do something against their will.

I drove past Mnumzane up to the drowsy rhino and, leaving the motor running, blocked his path with the vehicle. He could easily walk around us of course, so the plan was to keep moving in front of him, keeping him away from the rhino. We hoped he would get the message without feeling he had been interfered with—we didn't want to provoke a charge.

On Mnumzane came, until he was about ten paces away. Then he stopped and watched us guardedly, assessing the situation with his elephantine intelligence. As we predicted, he started to make a wide circle around the vehicle. Now came the tricky part, because not only would he be much closer, but he would realize he was being thwarted.

"Hold on," I said quietly, as I gently moved the Landy forward to block him.

Again he stopped, this time less than five yards away. Then he changed direction. I reversed, and as we started moving, his ears flared out and he swung to face us head-on. He had taken up the challenge. The tension ratcheted up as Mnumzane took an aggressive step toward us, his head held high.

"No! Mnumzane! No!" I called out the open window, ensuring that my voice conveyed intention rather than anger, or worse still, fear. "No!"

Again he stepped forward, ears belligerently splayed, tail up. This was no game.

"No, Mnumzane! No!" I called again, as I reversed in a tight semicircle to keep him away. "No!"

Out of the corner of my eye I saw the rhino wake up, stumble to her feet, and start to move off. I was relieved. We also now had more space to maneuver in. I swung the Landy around until we faced the temperamental elephant with about ten yards separating us.

Mnumzane began to swing his front foot, a sure sign that he was going to charge. Without thinking, I dropped the clutch and briefly lurched the Landy at him, and then again. I was challenging him directly.

"Whoa!" said David, gripping the dashboard. "Here he comes!"

We braced for the inevitable charge, but Mnumzane

suddenly broke and ran off at a gait, his trunk held high. I had to press home our advantage so I immediately followed him, goading him away until he reached thick bush and disappeared.

"That was a close one," said David, exhaling heavily. "I wouldn't try that with an adult bull."

He was absolutely right. Mnumzane's youth was on our side. It had worked, and the rhino was safe. We posted a ranger with the rhino and gave him instructions to call us if any elephants reappeared.

I went off to find Mnumzane and make my peace with him.

35

One night, a few months later, we were fast asleep when Bijou's growling woke us. Bijou, which means "jewel" in French, is Françoise's tiny Maltese poodle. Bijou enjoys a privileged life beyond anything Max or our other dog, Penny, could ever hope for. She gets the choice food—even steak—and sleeps on the bed between us.

Bijou was certainly not a watchdog, so when she started growling I knew something serious was going on.

I jumped out of bed and grabbed my shotgun. Suddenly I heard a heavy scraping sound on the roof, accompanied by soft thuds. The other dogs were also alert. Penny's hair stood stiff as wire on her back and she was crouching protectively next to Françoise. Max was sitting at the door, ears cocked but calm, watching me for instructions. Cautiously, I opened the top half of the door leading to the garden.

Whoa! A giant figure loomed up. I quickly stepped back, tripped over Max, staggered backward, slammed into the opposite wall, and then sprawled on the floor. Somehow I managed to keep the shotgun from hitting the wall and going off.

There, standing in the doorway, casually pulling the

grass from our thatched roof, was none other than Nana.

I could not believe my eyes. Of all the things that I could have imagined outside my front door in the middle of the night, a full-grown elephant was definitely not one of them.

I calmed down, got up, and walked toward the door. Not really knowing what to do, I began talking softly to Nana.

"Hey, Nana, you scared me. What are you doing here, you beautiful girl?"

I will always remember her response. She stretched out her trunk and I did likewise with my hand, as if it were the most natural thing in the world. For a few magnetic moments we connected. I stood a little closer, taking care to stay at the edge of her reach so she couldn't grab me, and she moved the tip of her trunk over my T-shirt and then touched me on the head and face. I held my ground, completely captivated by the exhilarating combination of danger and affection. Considering she couldn't see what she was doing because her eyes were above door level, she was surprisingly gentle.

She then lowered her head and moved forward, almost as if she were trying to come inside. With that, Bijou barked. And the spell was broken.

I doubt whether many people have had a ten-foot-tall, five-ton wild elephant try to squeeze her way into their house via a narrow door. Take it from me, it is not a relaxing experience.

Bijou and Penny went ballistic. They sprinted around the room barking like banshees. Surprised, Nana backed off a few paces and flared her ears.

Alarmed that the dogs were going to be stomped flat,

Françoise grabbed Penny and stuffed her into the bottom of a built-in closet. She then rushed after Bijou who, for reasons known only to her, was now shrieking at Max. I'm convinced that Nana was just too much for the tiny poodle to grasp, and so she turned on Max. As for Max, he just ignored her.

As Françoise was putting the semi-hysterical Bijou into the closet, Penny pushed open her door and came back into the fray. She wasn't going to let anything—not even an elephant—get between her and Françoise.

Françoise managed to scramble Penny into her arms again, but as she pushed her back in the closet, Bijou bolted out. It was an absolute circus. Eventually we locked all three dogs in the bathroom, and I was able to concentrate on Nana.

With all the commotion, she had moved off about ten paces, and only then I saw that the entire herd was with her. I looked at my watch. It was two a.m.

"This is amazing," I said to Françoise.

"What are they doing here?"

"I have no idea. But we might as well enjoy it while it lasts."

Enjoy it we did. There was an air of contentment as the animals strolled around the lawn in the moonlight, casting giant shadows across the garden.

As they moved off to the front of the house, I dashed across the lawn to the rangers' quarters to wake David. He had to see this. Then I rushed back to Françoise.

"You'd better wash," she said. She pointed at me with exaggerated revulsion on her face. I put my hand on my chest and was surprised to feel a gooey, sticky mess.

"Your head," Françoise said, wrinkling her nose. "It's all over your head."

I looked in the mirror and saw exactly what she was talking about. I was covered in elephant slime. I must have been wearing about half a pint of mucus from Nana's trunk.

"I'll wash later," I said. "David is joining us on the verandah. Let's go and watch."

I let Max out of the bathroom, and the three of us snuck to the rangers' house, keeping a sharp eye out for any stray jumbos. From the front verandah, Françoise watched the herd destroy her cherished garden. They pushed over trees, tore apart her favorite bushes, and ate every flower they could find.

David came out and joined us. "This is unbelievable. They're all here," he said, "except Mnumzane."

"No, he's here too," I said. "I saw him earlier."

Then David noticed him, standing alone in the dark about twenty yards away. "Poor guy," David said. "They tolerate him, but only just. I really hope he turns out okay."

"He's a big boy," I replied. "He'll be fine."

Nana looked up from the garden she was demolishing and, with a bunch of prized shrubs in her mouth, ambled over to us. Max, who had moved a few paces onto the lawn, silently retreated to the relative safety of the verandah and then followed Françoise when I suggested she go inside in case Nana got too close.

It was something I just couldn't get used to. That this gargantuan creature was apparently determined to demonstrate her affection by standing right next to me. What was even more mind-blowing was not that long ago she would have happily killed me.

Nana being overly friendly and nearly pushing me over with her trunk.

We decided to play it safe, so David and I moved back inside the double door and watched Nana's imposing bulk approach. She stopped at the low verandah wall and for the second time stretched out her trunk to me. She couldn't reach me, and I decided to hang back and watch and wait.

I underestimated her persistence, however—and her strength. Frustrated at my reluctance to come to her, she decided to come to me. She tried to squash her vast frame between the two brick pillars that straddled the verandah entrance. This obviously didn't work. We watched openmouthed as she then gently placed her forehead on the left pillar and gave an exploratory shove.

That certainly got my attention. Remembering what she had done to the gate poles at the *boma*, I had no doubt she would bring the whole verandah roof down if she wanted to. I quickly stepped forward. She stopped shoving the pillar and once again snaked her trunk over the top of my body. It was a good thing I hadn't washed yet, because I received another basting of slime. All the while, the sound of her deep rumbling reverberated through the house.

Once she was satisfied, Nana ambled away and joined the rest of the clan. Then suddenly, our eight-week-old kitten walked out onto the lawn, right where the herd was finishing off the few remaining exotic plants in Françoise's garden. We watched in horror. There was nothing we could do to help her. The elephants got very interested in this tiny thing and all sauntered over for a close inspection. Still, the tiny cat didn't react. I think these creatures were simply too big for her to take in, just as they had been for Bijou. The kitten was soon surrounded. The elephants waved the tips of their trunks around this tiny curiosity, and the kitten swiped at them playfully with her paw.

Eventually the elephants got tired of this, and they just walked off, leaving the kitten alone in the middle of the lawn.

Except for Frankie. At first she walked away, and then when she was about twenty yards off, she abruptly turned and ran at the kitten. It was a sight I don't think I will ever see again—a five-ton elephant charging a five-ounce cat.

The kitten finally realized something was wrong and skittered back to us just in time.

We stayed up watching the elephants until five a.m. Then, at the first hint of light, Nana moved off with the herd in tow. They soon disappeared in the dense bush.

I stared after them and felt a sense of emptiness. A part of me was leaving with them.

36

We went back to bed, and later that morning, I woke with a glorious glow of satisfaction. The herd's visit to our home demonstrated that we had made substantial progress. To think that not so long ago, I had been begging for the lives of seven angry, traumatized, human-hating pachyderms. Now I was trying to keep them out of our living room.

It seemed the rehabilitation of the herd was complete. All that was left was to celebrate our achievements. But whoever came up with the saying "pride comes before a fall" certainly knew what he was talking about.

I was enjoying a leisurely late breakfast, still thinking about Nana's extraordinary nocturnal display of affection, when I was bumped back to earth by a frantic call from the rangers.

"Mkhulu! *Mbomvu!* We are in danger! The elephants are chasing us. They are trying to kill us!"

It was Bheki, and I could hear the panic in his voice. He and the rangers were at the fence, near the river, many miles away on the other side of the reserve. The herd had certainly moved along quickly to be so far away from our house.

"How close are they?" I shouted into the radio.

"They are here. She is trying to kill us! The big ones want to kill us!"

Bheki is a highly experienced ranger, and the horror in his voice startled me. He is one of the toughest men I know.

"Get out, Bheki!" I yelled into the radio. "Take your men through the fence, cut it or find a place and go under."

Then I heard two shots over the radio.

"Bheki, what's happening? Who's shooting?"

"It's Ngwenya. He's shooting—" The radio went dead.

David, who had been listening, ran off and brought the Land Rover over, driving across Françoise's mutilated garden to our front door. I climbed in, and we sped for the gate.

The radio remained ominously silent for the forty minutes it took us to hurry across the reserve. We did not know what we would find.

Then about a hundred yards from the fence, I saw the herd milling about restlessly. On the other side, barely visible in the thick bush, Bheki and his men were huddling. I did a quick head count, first of the rangers, and then of the elephants, and exhaled deeply in absolute relief. Everyone was accounted for.

Frankie noticed us first. She angrily lifted her foot and stamped the ground until it trembled. She shook her mighty head. She was extremely agitated by whatever had happened and was letting us know it.

We pulled over and called out to the rangers, who cautiously emerged from the thicket, all eyes on the herd, which had now started to move off. I took out a pair of pliers, snipped the fence, and lifted the electric wires with a stick so they could crawl back into the reserve.

"You were lucky," I said as I fixed the fence. "Now you have seen up close how dangerous these elephants are. Tell the others—tell everyone working here—to keep their eyes open and stay far away from them."

I knew this episode would quickly spread through the village, with huge exaggerations. I hoped the stories would further discourage potential poachers.

But that was not my main concern. What really alarmed me was that the herd had had no obvious reason to charge the rangers. Either the animals had been accidentally provoked by Bheki and his men or they were just determined to rid their new territory of all humans they did not know. Perhaps the guards with their rifles reminded them of poachers from their earlier lives.

The more I thought about it, however, the more I believed the real reason was probably simpler. The rangers had most likely been casually chatting, not paying attention to where they were. Before they realized it, they must have stumbled into the elephants' space and then were in deep trouble. Or at least that's what I hoped had happened. We would never know, but it was clear that this was still an extremely dangerous herd. There was a lot of work to be done before we could really relax. If we ever could.

37

I spent time with the herd every day, not only to check on their habits and movements, but because it was so invigorating to be out there with them. Most important, I wanted to continue to investigate some aspects of their communication that intrigued me.

I was on foot searching for elephants one hot afternoon, when for a split second I got the feeling that the herd was right there. I quickly looked around, but they were nowhere in sight.

A little later, it happened again. It was the lightest sensation, and then it was gone. Again I looked around, but there was still no sign of them. Something was going on. I was surprised I had never noticed anything like this before.

So I waited, going back to doing exactly what I had been doing before, just being part of the bush, not expecting anything to happen. All of a sudden, I got it again: that strong sense that the herd was close by. With that, Nana emerged out of a nearby thicket followed by the others. I was stunned. I had somehow picked up that they were there long before I saw or heard them.

In time I discovered that I also had this experience in reverse. Sometimes while searching for the elephants I would eventually realize that they were not in the area at all, not because I couldn't find them but because the bush felt completely empty of their presence.

After a couple of weeks, I started getting the hang of it. Eventually it became easier and easier to find the herd. Somehow, elephants project their presence into an area around them, and they have control over this, because when they didn't want to be found I could be almost on top of them and not sense that at all.

After a little more experimentation, I think I figured out what was happening. The herd's deep rumblings, which are well below human hearing, were resonating in the bush for miles around them. Even though I couldn't hear the rumblings at all, I must have been sensing them on some level.

One morning while driving along a boulder-strewn track, I sensed that elephants were around. Then I heard a distinct trumpeting. I stopped, and a few minutes later I heard it again, this time much closer. A breathless Mnumzane lumbered out of the woodland and stopped right in front of the Land Rover, cutting me off. He stared intently at me through the windshield. He had never come that close before.

Mnumzane was absolutely calm, but I sat there in the vehicle, my heart beating loudly. Twenty minutes later, he was still there, browsing all around the Landy and showing no signs of leaving, and I was much more relaxed.

Then the radio squawked to life, and Mnumzane tensed at the invasion of sound. It was the office, requesting that I return to base. But as I started to pull off, Mnumzane quickly moved in front of the vehicle. Without any nastiness, he deliberately blocked the way. Puzzled, I switched off the Land Rover, and he casually returned to his grazing. As soon as I keyed the ignition again, he got in my way once more. He relaxed only when I switched off the motor.

It was clear he didn't want me to leave. I rolled the window down.

"Hello, big boy. What's up today?"

He slowly, almost hesitantly, came around to the window. He stood a yard or so away, looking down at me with his wise brown eyes. He rolled his head leisurely and seemed completely content, radiating easy companionship. I felt as though I were in the presence of an old friend.

What intrigued me were the feelings, like this one, that I experienced when I was with the elephants. It seemed to be their feelings, not mine. The elephants determined the emotional tone of any encounter. This is what Mnumzane was

My beautiful big boy Mnumzane arriving for a bush chat. Look at the size of him: I am 6'3" and only come up to his tusks.

doing at this very moment, passing on the sensation of being with an old friend.

It dawned on me that Mnumzane had chosen me for company over his own kind. That was why he had trumpeted out to tell me to wait when I drove past him. That was why he wouldn't let me leave now.

I felt absolutely humbled. The hairs on my arm were stiff with goose bumps as this colossus towered above me, so obviously wanting to be friends. I decided to make the most of the experience—or rather, privilege—and stayed put.

He continued feeding and moved from one tree to the next. He snapped branches like twigs and stripped the leaves. Every now and again, he would lift his massive head and unfurl his trunk at me, sniffing to make sure I was still there.

After about another thirty minutes, he turned and stepped aside to let my vehicle through.

"Thank you, Mnumzane. See you tomorrow, my friend."

He tilted his head for a moment and then, with that peculiar, graceful, swaying gait, melted into the bush.

38

As I spent more time with Nana and her charges, they too started coming closer and closer until they were happy to graze near the Land Rover. I was watching them on one occasion when Nana suddenly stopped feeding and walked up to the vehicle.

I didn't move. I could sense that she was being friendly so I didn't feel threatened. But I was totally unprepared for what happened next. Infinitely slowly, or so it felt, she stretched her trunk through the window to greet me. It was shockingly intimate, and although she had touched me before—both at the *boma* and when she came up to the house—I believe this was the elephantine equivalent of an affectionate pat. She was letting me know that she was fine with me being out there with them on their turf. Despite the obviously dangerous circumstances, I had never felt more comfortable, nor more at ease.

Even Frankie was becoming friendlier. She would stand quite close to the vehicle with Mabula and Marula. The battle-ax had a soft side, and once, she even started to reach out with her trunk. But as soon as I put my hand up, she lost her nerve and withdrew.

Despite the feel-good factor, I never forgot that these were wild elephants. Whenever they came close I continuously moved the Land Rover to make sure I would never be cut off or put in a situation where I felt uncomfortable or, worse, trapped.

These encounters gradually became more and more spontaneous. As the months went by, I started getting individual greetings from the rest of the herd. They didn't go as far as putting their trunks in the car as Nana did, but they would come right up and lift their trunks as if waving to me. What they were doing, of course, was smelling me. I seemed to have been accepted as an honorary member of the group.

In the process, the Land Rover was taking a beating. Elephants are always touching, pushing, and brushing against each other. Being accepted by them meant that my Land Rover was getting bumped all the time. The hefty jumbos left crater-size dents in the vehicle. The Landy eventually looked as though it had been in a particularly eventful NASCAR race. It attracted a lot of attention on my trips to town and was quickly nicknamed "the elephant car."

The herd also loved to play with anything that stuck out or up on the vehicle. My sideview mirrors were yanked off as if they were made of paper. Both radio antennas went the same way. I replaced them with screw-on antennas, which I could remove before I went out to meet the herd. The windshield wipers were stripped off so frequently that I gave up replacing them. I just drove with my head out of the window if it rained.

For some reason, they found the texture of metal fascinating. They would spend hours feeling it. They also loved the heat pinging off the engine, especially if the weather was cold. They would rest their trunks on the hood for long periods. In summer when the hood was searing hot, they would lay their trunks down on it, then quickly yank them off. And they would do it again just a few minutes later.

Because every week or two they came up to the house, we eventually strung an electric wire around Françoise's garden. Otherwise, they would have trampled it flat and gobbled up the shrubbery. They would stand patiently at the wire until I came down and said hello.

One week I went to Durban on business. When I returned, I was surprised to see all seven elephants outside the house. They looked like a welcome-home committee. I thought it was just a coincidence. But it happened again after the next trip, and the next one after that. It soon became obvious that somehow they knew exactly when I was away and when I was coming back.

Then it got . . . well, spooky. I was at the airport in Johannesburg and missed my flight home. I was later told that back at Thula Thula, four hundred miles away, the herd was on their way up to the house when they suddenly halted, turned around, and retreated into the bush. We later worked out that this happened at exactly the time I missed my flight.

The next day they were back at the house when I arrived.

39

One day David said worriedly, "We can't find the elephants anywhere. If we hadn't checked the fences, I would swear they've broken out."

"Nah. They're happy here," I said. "Those breakout days are gone."

"Maybe." He shrugged. "But where are they?"

An image of Nana the last time I had seen her suddenly flashed through my mind. Her belly had been as swollen as a barrel. I knew that both she and Frankie had been impregnated by the head bull at their previous reserve.

An elephant is pregnant for twenty-two months, and Nana and Frankie were near the end of their pregnancies. During that time they had gone through so much, including the death of their matriarch, a change in home, and a breakout from Thula Thula.

I figured that at least one of them must have gone deep into the bush to give birth. I loaded up the Land Rover with a day's supplies and set off to search as far into the densest parts of Thula Thula's wilderness as I could get. But I couldn't find any fresh signs of the herd whatsoever. I looked in all the lush feeding areas and their favorite hidey-holes. There was no trace of them. The world's largest land mammals had seemingly vanished into thin air.

Finally in the early afternoon, I noticed some fresh tracks in an area we call Zulu Graves. It's a two-hundred-year-old burial ground that dates back to the days of King Shaka, the founder of the Zulu nation.

"Coooome, Nana!" I called out, singing the words in the tone the elephants were now used to. "Coooome, my *babbas* . . ." They always seemed to respond to this Zulu word for "babies."

Soon the bush started to move, alive with the unmistakable sound of elephants. I experienced the mixture of thrill, fear, and affection I had every time I was in their presence. I called out again, high on anticipation.

"Coooome, *babbas*?"

Then I saw Nana. She was standing well off the dirt road, watching me but reluctant to get near. That's strange, I thought. She normally comes closer.

She hesitated for some time, neither coming forward nor retreating into the bush. She seemed uncertain about what to do. Then I saw why. Standing next to her was a perfectly formed baby elephant. The baby stood about two and a half feet high and was maybe just a few days old. I was looking at the first elephant to be born in our area in over one hundred years.

I didn't want to intrude. I stood there with my heart pounding. Then Nana took a few steps forward, then a few more, and finally she started walking slowly toward me with the baby tottering alongside on its tiny unsteady feet, its little trunk bobbing like a piece of elastic.

She was still about thirty yards away when suddenly Frankie appeared with her ears flared. It was a stark signal for me to back off. I jumped into the Land Rover and reversed to create a safe zone. Then I switched off the motor and watched.

Gradually the rest of the herd came out of the bush. They eyed me cautiously and milled around Nana and the baby.

I watched enthralled as they continually touched and caressed the little one. Even Mnumzane was partially involved. He stood at the periphery as close as he was allowed and watched the goings-on.

Then Nana, who had been facing me, started to walk up the road. I quickly got in, slammed the vehicle into reverse, and edged farther back, acutely aware of the engraved-in-stone bush rule that you don't go anywhere near an elephant and her baby. But she kept coming. I figured they wanted to use the road, so I reversed off at a right angle into the long grass to allow them to pass well in front of me.

To my absolute surprise, Nana left the road and followed me, with Frankie and the others just a few yards behind. I was no longer in her way so there was no need for this—they could have just strolled past. Nana had made a conscious decision to come after me, and my heart started thumping overtime. I quickly shoved Max off the front seat onto the floor and threw my jacket over him. "Stay, boy," I said as he settled down. "We have visitors."

Squinting hard into the sun, I tried to detect any hint of hostility, any edginess that I was intruding in matters maternal. There was none, not even from fierce-tempered and still-very-pregnant Frankie. All around, the bush breathed peace. It was as if a group decision had been made to approach me.

Nana ambled up to my window and stood towering above the Land Rover, dominating the skyline. Below her was her baby. Incredibly, she had brought her newborn to me.

I held my breath as Nana's trunk reached into the Land Rover and touched me on the chest. Its sandpapery hide was somehow as delicate as silk. Then her trunk swiveled back, dropped and touched the little one. It was a pachyderm introduction. I sat still, stunned by the privilege she was bestowing on me.

"You clever girl," I said, my voice scratchy. "What a magnificent baby."

Her massive skull, just a few yards from mine, seemed to swell even larger with pride.

"I don't know what you call him. But he was born during the first spring showers, so I will call him *Mvula*."

Mvula is the Zulu word for "rain," synonymous with life for those who live with the land. She seemed to agree, and the name stuck.

Then she slowly moved off, leading the herd back the way they had come. Within minutes they'd evaporated into the bush.

Two weeks later they disappeared again, and I made another trek to Zulu Graves. They were there, at exactly the same place as before. This time it was Frankie with a perfect new baby. I went through the same backing-off procedure to ensure I didn't invade their space. Eventually Frankie, too, came to me, herd in tow. However, she didn't stop like Nana had. She just walked past the vehicle to show off her infant.

"Well done, my beautiful girl," I said as she slowly came level with the window, her maternal pride in full bloom. "We will call him *Ilanga*—the sun."

I shook my head in wonderment. A little over a year ago she had almost killed Françoise and me on the quad bike. Now she was proudly parading her baby. It blew my mind just thinking about it. We had traveled a long road together.

That evening they all came up to the house. Frankie's little one was only one week old but she had walked nearly four miles through thick bush. This time Frankie stood in front of the others, right at the wire facing me.

"Hello, girl. Your baby is so beautiful! She really is!"

Frankie stood caressing her calf, visibly glowing with pride. All the while she looked directly at me. This was the closest we had come to connecting with each other. We both knew something precious had passed between us.

These almost-unbelievable experiences had a sequel several years later when my first grandson was born, and the herd came up to the house. I took baby Ethan in my arms and went as near to the patiently waiting elephants as his worried mother would allow. They were only a few yards away. Their trunks went straight up and they all edged closer, intensely focused on the little bundle in my arms. They smelled the air to get the baby's scent and they rumbled excitedly.

I was repaying the compliment to them, introducing them, trusting them with my baby as they had trusted me with theirs.

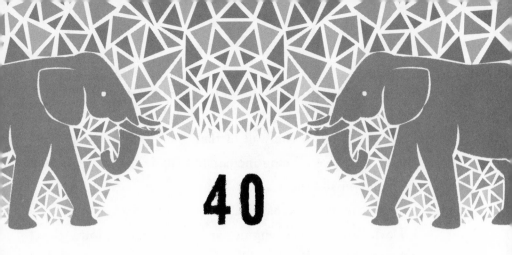

40

One day a fire started on the far side of the reserve. Four hot, sooty hours later, the flaming monster ripped through the bush completely out of control. I realized with horror that we were fighting for the life of Thula Thula itself.

The rangers and I piled into the Land Rover and David sped off, just yards in front of the flames. There was only one road out of the area, but as long as David kept the gas pedal on the floor of the Landy, perhaps we could make it.

As we raced for our lives, I searched the bush for any sign of the elephants. The fire could not have come at a worse time for Nana and Frankie with their two new babies. I was terrified they would be trapped. As the situation worsened, I could think of little else.

At this point, the road took us parallel to the advancing fire, which was now a mile wide, flaring and roaring and leaping on our right, drowning us in toxic fumes and swirling tendrils of smoldering ash.

"The elephants came through here!" shouted David above the crackling of the flames. He pointed to fresh elephant dung.

"They stopped here!" I shouted back. "Probably to rest

the babies, but more so, I think, to let Nana assess the situation. I think she is trying to get to Croc Pools."

I looked back at the wall of flames and felt my stomach tighten. Trees were being incinerated whole. Nothing in its path could possibly survive.

"Please make it, Nana," I said under my breath.

David gunned the engine, and we bounced down the track as fast as we could.

"Where to?" yelled David. "Hurry, or else we've had it!"

In a flash, I realized what we had to do. Nana had shown us the way.

"Croc Pools!" I shouted back. "If Nana thinks it's safe enough for the herd, it'll be safe enough for us."

Somehow, in the blinding smoke David found the turnoff, and ten bumpy minutes later we rounded the corner at the pools just as Nana was shepherding the last of her charges into deep water. She and Frankie stood in the shallow water with the babies, Mvula and Ilanga, and made sure the others were safe.

Only then did I understand why they were there. It was not just because of the water. The grass around every game reserve pool is always overgrazed because so many animals visit the water to drink. This meant there would be little grass to fuel the fire in a thirty-yard radius around the Croc Pools.

Clever, clever girl, I thought.

We drove to the opposite side and maneuvered the Land Rover into a spot as close to the pools as we could. We splashed water over the vehicle to cool it down and then waded knee-deep into the pool. The coolness and relief was exquisite.

There is a reason why this particular stretch is called Croc Pools. I looked around hurriedly. There were two huge crocodiles lying still in the shallow reed beds to our left. They watched us through their hooded, reptilian eyes. Fortunately, because of the fire, the last thing on their minds right now was lunch. We would be fine where we were. For good measure, though, I reached down and grabbed Max's collar tightly.

And there we were in the Croc Pools: a herd of elephants, two crocodiles, a dog, and a sweaty group of men united by the most basic instinct of all—survival.

41

As the fire approached, we watched yellow-billed kites soar and swoop down on seared insects fleeing the flames. Flocks of glossy starlings darted in and out of the smoke doing the same thing. Two large monitor lizards came hurtling out of the bush and splashed headlong into the water next to us. Then a herd of zebras came galloping out of the fumes and stopped. The stallion sniffed the air, then changed direction and sped off with his family. They would outrun the fire.

Thick smoke from the burning bush poured over us, blocking out all sunlight. Then it was on us, the heat sizzling and hissing across the water. I suddenly felt Nana's rumblings. They were a dominating, calming presence. There she stood, shielding the babies with her body and spraying water over herself. I found myself doing the same, scooping water over my head as if I had joined the herd.

And then the fire swept past, and the sun broke through. We stared out at the blackened landscape, gulping air into our smoke-seared lungs. We had made it, thanks to Nana. She had saved us all.

Meanwhile, on the other side of the reserve, all the

remaining staff were working to protect the lodge and hou

Just as it seemed the thatched lodge and our homes were about to be engulfed in flames, a bunch of four-wheel drives loaded with firefighting equipment came revving through the smoke down the road. Every nearby farmer and his truck had come to help.

Thirty minutes later the fire was finally out. It was now a mere mopping-up operation. But the fire had destroyed more than one third of the reserve.

Fortunately that night, a torrent of refreshing rain washed clean the charred, blackened earth.

The next morning, elephants, rhinos, zebras, impalas, and other animals were out on the burned areas. They were eating fresh ash, something wildlife always does after a fire. The ash apparently has salts and minerals that their bodies crave.

Two weeks later, the areas that had been so badly burned were emerald green. Thanks to the fire, we now had thousands of acres of new flourishing grassland.

42

I had wanted the elephants to get used to vehicles, and it had worked. The elephants now moved about unconcerned, not only when I drove up to them, but also when Land Rovers filled with our lodge guests came near them. Of course, our rangers kept the vehicles a reasonable distance away and respected the elephants' privacy.

Now I wanted to interact with Nana and her family on foot. For the safety of our rangers and other workers, it was important to get the herd used to humans walking around in the bush. Plus, I planned to introduce walking safaris as an attraction for our guests.

I took Max with me and drove off for my first experiment. I found the herd grazing in an open area. There were plenty of big trees nearby I could climb if something went wrong and I had to run for it.

I pulled over next to a spreading marula and got out. I left the Landy's door open just in case I needed to leave in a hurry. Communicating with elephants out in the open, on foot, is vastly different from doing so from a vehicle.

I purposely went upwind so they could get my scent. I

zigzagged toward the elephants, ambling along as if on a Sunday stroll, Max by my side. Everything went fine until I was about thirty yards away from them. Then Frankie's trunk swiveled near the ground and she got my scent. She peered at Max and me, and I stopped immediately. After a tense minute, she chose to ignore us and resumed feasting. So far so good. I continued to move in their general direction.

I was just five paces closer when Frankie suddenly lifted her head sharply and aggressively spread her ears.

Whoa! I stopped again. This time, though, she continued glaring at me until I backed off five or six paces. That seemed to satisfy her, and she went back to grazing.

I repeated this several times over the next hour. I would go a few paces in and always get the same angry reaction. So I would move back and be ignored again. That's interesting, I thought. Frankie has created a boundary. When I am outside it, I am welcome. When I am inside it, she gets irritable.

I checked the distance to the Land Rover to make sure I could reach it if I needed to, and then I pushed through the imaginary boundary and came closer.

Frankie swung around and took three aggressive steps toward me with her trunk held high. I backed off—fast.

I got into the Land Rover with Max and drove around to where Nana was grazing. The same thing happened, except that Nana let me get much closer than Frankie did. And when I crossed Nana's boundary, she seemed more annoyed than aggressive.

Over the next weeks, through trial and error, I learned

that the herd set a very real, if invisible, boundary inside of which no human could enter. I also learned that every elephant's space is different. I discovered, too, that the smaller the elephant, the less confident they are and, therefore, they demand more space around them. A mother and newborn baby need the most space of all.

To have walking safaris on Thula Thula, I needed the herd to be completely comfortable, otherwise the risk was not worth it. I needed to do more research, so I did my experiment again, but this time with Vusi, a fast-moving young ranger, who bravely volunteered. All he had to do was walk slowly around the herd while I watched their reactions. I estimated the herd's safety boundary, told Vusi where it was, dropped him off, and told him to walk.

Big mistake. Frankie bristled on full alert right after Vusi started. He legged it back to the Landy quicker than an Olympic runner.

Vusi did a little more experimenting, and it became clear that, as far as the herd was concerned, the boundary with a stranger was much, much wider than it was with me.

How could I get the elephants to draw the boundary in? I thought that if my own boundary was closer, then the boundary for strangers could be closer, too. So I started hanging around the edges of the boundary, minding my own business. Then I slowly tried to move a bit closer. The key to this was patience. It took endless hours of just being there. I also found that if I ignored them or faced away from them, I attracted less attention.

Although it was a tiresome exercise, it was also an extremely tense one. I had to be constantly ready to dash off in a split second.

As time passed, I was making zero progress and beginning to despair. Even Mnumzane would not come closer while he was with the herd. Then one day, Nana ambled over in my direction to reach a small tree she decided to eat. By doing so, she shrank the boundary by half without even looking up at me. A short while later, Frankie and the others joined her.

Then it dawned on me. The herd's boundary was not set in stone. It could be reset, but only by the elephants when they were good and ready. It had to be their decision.

I learned another important rule: Never approach the elephants directly. Rather, put yourself in their vicinity, and if they want to, they will come closer. If not, forget it.

During this time, young Mandla charged me repeatedly. He was now a healthy two-and-a-half-year-old, almost four feet tall. He would put his ears out and run at me for about five or six yards. Then he'd bolt back to the safety of his mother, Nana. She kept an eye on things but always ignored his "heroic" antics.

Mandla's charging toward me became a great game between us. Every day I would call out and talk to him as he put on his show, and we would have fun. He got braver and braver and came closer and closer. I had to be very careful. He was big enough to seriously hurt me, but this was never anything but a fun game.

One day Nana and Mvula were a little way from the herd

when Nana slowly started walking in my direction. Good Lord! Had she decided to come all the way over to me? Unless I bolted before she got any closer, I would be stuck out in the open without any escape route whatsoever. This was an entirely different ballgame than being approached by her when I was in the Land Rover.

Nana lumbered on in such a friendly way that I steeled myself and decided to stay and see what happened. I was also gambling that the rest of the elephants would stay away.

Closer and closer she came, with Mvula scampering at her heels. I glanced nervously down at Max, who was watching keenly, completely still. He looked up at me and wagged his tail. He hadn't sensed anything dangerous. I hoped he was right, because there was a very big elephant coming toward us.

Suddenly some survival instinct kicked in and competed with my decision to stand fast. The need to flee this colossus exploded within me. I could scarcely breathe, but I was determined not to run. It was all I could do to hold my ground. To this day I don't know how I managed not to bolt. But stay I did. And then there she was, her huge form towering above me, blocking out the sky.

I think she sensed my fear because she stopped about five yards away and simply started to graze again. She was oozing calm and peace. When you are standing five yards away from a wild, five-ton elephant you are acutely aware of every little thing around you, especially the elephant's emotional state.

Somehow I had enough presence of mind to recognize how unusual it was to stand out on an open plain with a matriarch and her baby. But there was such an innocence about our spontaneous get-together that it helped me keep my dignity and hold my ground.

Five minutes later, Nana was still there. I realized we were actually hanging out together. She moved around slowly, grazing, and I relaxed enough to notice that she had the most graceful table manners. Her trunk searched out and skillfully encircled a chosen clod of grass, which she would pluck and delicately tap on her knee to dislodge soil from the roots. Then she placed the greens inside her mouth, leaving just the roots protruding. A gentle clamp of her molars and the roots were severed. And she would enjoy her morsel. I noticed too that she was very fussy about what she ate. She checked the scent of each plant before she decided if she wanted to devour it.

Watching her eat trees was no less fascinating. She easily removed the leaves from a young acacia, placed them in her mouth, and then snapped off a branch. As soon as she had finished chewing the leaves, the branch went in one side of her mouth and, a little while later, was ejected out the other. The branch would be stripped of all bark, the only part she was after.

All the while Mvula peeked at Max and me from behind his mother's tree-trunk legs, occasionally stepping out to get a better look. Max sat silently. He occasionally moved a few yards to smell where Nana had been standing, but otherwise he stayed motionless.

I was intensely focused on this magnificent creature standing so close to me. All the while Nana kept glancing or staring at me. Every now and then she would turn her massive body slightly toward me, or move her ears just a touch in my direction. Her occasional deep rumblings vibrated through my body.

So this was how she communicated: with her eyes, trunk, rumblings, subtle body movements, and, of course, her attitude. I finally got it. She was trying to get through to me—and, like an idiot, I hadn't been responding at all.

I looked directly at Nana and said, "Thank you." I was acknowledging her to test her reaction. The effect was immediate. She glanced across and held my gaze for several deep seconds before she returned contentedly to her grazing. It was almost as if she were saying, "Didn't you see me? What took you so long?"

The final piece of the puzzle clicked perfectly into place. While I had been standing there, she had been trying to get me to accept her presence. She wanted me to give her some sign that I recognized her. Yet I had been as stiff and rigid as a plank. When I finally acknowledged her, with a simple thank-you, she instantly responded.

That "eureka" moment with Nana really drove home to me the essence of communicating with any animal. Whether it is a pet dog or a wild elephant, communication is not so much about the reach as it is about the acknowledgment. It's the acknowledgment that does it. In the animal kingdom, communication is a two-way street, just as it is with humans. If you are not letting them know that their communication has reached you, if you don't acknowledge it somehow, there can be *no* communication. It's as simple as that.

Me and Françoise with our little princess, Bijou, at the lodge.

Nana.

The herd under a beautiful sky.

Mnumzane and friend moving past the lodge.

Frankie and baby Ilanga leading young Mabula and Marula.

The herd bathing in the Gwala Gwala Dam.

Nkosi [Chief] Phiwayinkosi Chakide Biyela in full traditional regalia.

Mabula at a watering hole.

Eye movements are perhaps the most important form of communication. A flick of the eye, a look, or the tiniest glance may seem like nothing to humans, but in the animal world it's a very big deal. Attitude, facial expressions (believe me, elephants can smile beautifully), and body language can also be significant.

So how do you acknowledge them? Just a look can be enough. Or simply using words in the tone you would naturally use to convey your feelings can also achieve a lot.

There are other factors, of course. Animals have an amazing ability to pick up on your state of mind, especially if you are hostile. All it takes to make progress communicating with an animal is an open mind. With some patience and persistence everything will eventually click into place. The best part is that you will recognize it when it happens. Anyone can do it, and as many people already know, it is so worthwhile. Communication is not exclusive to humans; it is truly universal.

I looked up to see Frankie leading the rest of the herd to me. There was no way I was going to risk that sort of interaction. I left in a hurry, after I thanked Nana. I also told her I would see her again soon. It would be an understatement to say I was deeply humbled by the experience.

43

After Nana let me "hang out" with her and Mvula, everything changed. It was now easy to be around the entire herd. Even Vusi could walk reasonably close to them. One day I had four rangers stroll past the elephants as if they were on a game walk and . . . we had done it! Even Frankie didn't raise an eyebrow.

Nana had obviously communicated to the rest of the herd her decision to accept us. From that I learned another important lesson. Previously traumatized wild elephants appeared to regain a degree of faith in new humans once the matriarch has established trust with just one human. And it must be the matriarch. My close relationship with Mnumzane hadn't altered the herd's attitude toward me one little bit.

Now, thanks to Nana, guests of Thula Thula could walk in the wild near her family. This was an experience to be savored for a lifetime. I marveled that barely two years earlier Frankie had tried to kill the manager of the Umfolozi reserve while he was tracking them during their breakout.

One evening, when the lodge was full and a candlelit dinner was being served to guests on the verandah, Nana suddenly appeared on the lawn right in front of the lodge, the herd in tow.

Wow, she is a bit close, I thought as I watched her movements carefully. Were they headed for the nearby watering hole?

"Elephant, elephant!" shouted two first-timers. They were immediately shushed by more seasoned bush lovers, while others grabbed for cameras. The whole herd came into view. It was a great game-viewing experience but, I quickly realized, they were not going to the watering hole, after all. They were coming toward the lodge.

The lodge at Thula Thula.

Elephants operate on the firm principle that all other life-forms must give way to them. As far as they were concerned, tourists at a sit-down dinner around a swimming pool were no different from a troop of baboons at a watering hole.

Nana came toward us without breaking a step. I waited

until I knew that she was definitely not going to stop or change course, and then I whispered loudly to the guests, "Let's go! Go, go!"

Most of the guests rushed into the lodge for cover, but one group stayed exactly where they were. They lounged with great exaggeration over the dining chairs and pretended to be indifferent to the nearing herd.

Frankie looked up and flicked her ears at the group. Unable to recognize the customary warning, the group stayed put. Not getting the appropriate response, Frankie took a few quick steps toward them, her trunk held high and her ears flared like a cape.

"She's charging!" someone shouted. Then chaos erupted. Chairs went flying everywhere as the group blindly ran into each other in their desperate attempt to flee.

Satisfied that she had gotten the respect she deserved from this naughty group of primates, Frankie dropped her ears and fell back in line behind Nana. They all ambled across the lawn and up onto the lodge's tiled game-viewing patio. They stood huge and imposingly out of place, looking at their surroundings.

The coast was clear. Attracted by the strange things on the fully decorated dining table, the elephants moved over to explore. Glasses and plates were swept aside by careless trunks and smashed all over the place. Similarly, candles and holders were tossed on the floor. Then the tablecloth was violently yanked from below the remaining crockery and cutlery, completing the destruction.

When the elephants discovered that some of the mess was in fact edible, they delicately picked up and ate every bread roll and all the salad from the floor. They walked over glass shards as if they were paper. The table was roughly shoved aside, cracking open as it moved. I watched in amazement as first one chair then another went airborne. Tiring of the dinner, the herd now focused on the real purpose of their visit—the swimming pool.

That's what they're here for, I thought. They know about the pool. I bet they've been here before, probably late at night.

The swimming pool was apparently the elephants' new watering hole. All Nana was doing was simply clearing the guests away, just as she would any other animal. The herd wanted to drink in peace.

Nana dropped her huge trunk into the pool and sucked gallons of the sparkling clear water up her trunk. Then she threw her head back and delivered the water messily to her gaping mouth and gave the rumbling go-ahead to the others.

They had an absolute ball. Mvula, Ilanga, and Mandla, to the delight of the now-peeking guests, cavorted around, slipping on the tiles. The larger animals drank their fill and bathed themselves with huge squirts and sprays from their trunks.

Everything was sort of going well until Nana picked up my scent. She slowly swung around and lumbered toward where I was standing next to a thatch pole just inside the lodge patio. I held my ground as she lifted the tip of her dripping-wet trunk across my chest. This show of affection was understandably misinterpreted by several of the guests, who, certain of my impending death, bolted silently for the safety of the bathroom.

"Clever girl!" I said. "You found the cleanest water on the reserve. And managed to scare everyone in the process," I added, with just a touch of discipline in my voice.

I took a step forward and raised my hand to the body of her trunk and caressed her. "But you really are frightening the guests, and you do need to leave now."

Nana decided otherwise. Five minutes later she was still standing there peacefully, while in the background Frankie stared and flicked her ears at any guest who so much as moved from their hiding place.

Nana really needed to go. A lodge full of tourists certainly wasn't the place for her and her family to visit. So I took my leave of her. I backed off three or four paces under the thatch, clapped my hands lightly and encouraged her to move off.

Well, she didn't like that at all. She moved forward, leaned her head on the support pole in front of me, and gave it a heave. With that, the lodge's entire roof shifted. Controlling my urge to shout, I quickly moved forward and began to stroke Nana's trunk and speak soothingly to her again. Incredibly she leaned forward again, this time with more force. Judging by the groaning sound of the building's wooden supports, it seemed that the whole structure was on the verge of collapsing.

I instinctively did the only thing I could. I put both hands high on her trunk and pushed back on her with all my strength, pleading with her not to destroy our livelihood.

And there we stayed, her leaning on the pole and me pushing on her. It was the longest thirty seconds of my life. Finally she stepped back, shook her head at me, and walked away. She took a huge dump on the patio to show her disgust.

It was all a game, of course. Nana could have collapsed the pole easily, and my puny effort to push her off was nothing stronger than a feather in the wind. She was just making a point.

The rest of the herd followed Nana as she walked down onto the lawn and eventually moseyed into the bush.

The next morning, we put up a single electric strand around the lodge grounds, at adult-elephant-head height. To keep Nana happy, we also set up a new drinking trough right outside the wire that we filled with water from an underground well.

This arrangement works well. Even if the electric wire is down, they never try to come to the lodge.

44

"Can you take another elephant?" Marion Garaï of the EMOA asked me on the phone early one morning. "I've got a fourteen-year-old female that desperately needs a home. Her entire family has been shot or sold, and she's completely alone on a reserve. Even worse, she's been sold to a trophy hunter."

She delivered this last bit almost as an aside, but she knew it would get me going like nothing else. Trophy hunting was something I simply could not understand: What type of person would shoot a terrified teenage elephant? And what kind of reserve owner would sell her in the first place?

I have never had a problem with hunting for the pot. Every living thing on this planet hunts for food one way or another. Survival of the fittest is, like it or not, the way of this world. But hunting for pleasure—killing only for the thrill of it—is to me an abomination.

I thought about how Nana and her clan would feel about a new elephant in their midst. Because they now seemed so settled, I was pretty confident the herd would accept another young female into the family. So I agreed to take her, and

Marion told me she had a donor who would pay the hunter back and all costs to get the elephant to Thula Thula.

We hurriedly repaired the *boma*, and David and I and another ranger named Brendan prepared for a stint in the bush while our new arrival got settled. We even parked the Land Rover in the same position as David and I had when the original herd was in quarantine.

The transport truck arrived mid-afternoon and backed into the loading trench. This time we had the levels right and the loading bay opened smoothly. We all craned forward for a good look. But as soon as the truck's door opened, the youngster sprinted straight into the thickest part of the *boma*'s bush, where she hid for the next few days. She came out only in the dead of night to eat the food we had tossed over the fence. Whenever we tried to get closer, she bolted to the far side. I have never witnessed such terror in an animal. There was no doubt she thought we were going to kill her, just as humans had killed the rest of her family.

Using the techniques I had developed with the herd, I started to talk to her gently. I walked around singing and whistling, trying to get her used to me as a friendly presence. But no matter what I did, she remained petrified and stayed in the densest part of the thicket.

After nearly a week, there was no change in her. I decided I needed to do something different. So I walked up to the fence, picked a spot, and just stayed there. I didn't talk or do anything except pointedly ignore her. I just stood there.

Each morning and each afternoon I chose a different

spot and moved a tiny bit closer to her hiding place each time.

On the third day this prompted a reaction, but instead of being soothed, she came out of the bush furiously, charging like a whirlwind at me.

I watched her come, amazed. I had thought such a lost soul would respond to warmth. The *boma*'s electric fence was between us, and I knew I was not in any real danger. I also knew I had three choices: I could stand firm and show her who was boss. I could ignore her. Or I could back off.

I sensed that her charge lacked seriousness. This poor creature—a couple of tons of tusk and flesh that could kill me with a single swipe—seemed to have the self-confidence of a mouse. She needed to believe in herself, to know she deserved respect and was a master of the wilderness. She needed to believe she had won the encounter. So I backed off with some major theatrics. I decided to let her know that, in this instance, she was the boss.

She pulled up at the fence in a cloud of dust and stared, dumbfounded. She had probably never seen a human run away before.

She watched my retreat and then swiveled and ran back into the thicket with her trunk held high in victory. It was the first time I had witnessed her do that. She had seen off an enemy. More important, she had turned fear into action, which, for the moment at least, was a huge improvement.

It worked well, almost too well. She now started charging whenever I came close. Each time I played the game, pretending to be afraid and backing right off. I wanted to show her how powerful she was, that she was queen of the bush. Elephants are majestic. They are not bullies or cowards. I had to let her rediscover herself.

She slowly started to get her nerve back and even began coming out into the open during the day and wandering around the *boma*.

Whenever she came out of the thicket, I tried to make sure I was around. She watched me with beady eyes as I once more started to talk and sing to her at random, alternating that with being there quietly. She never uttered a sound, whether she was interested, angry, or frightened. To me this was uniquely sad. A trumpeting elephant is bush music. Yet this distraught creature was silent, even when coming at me full tilt.

Then one day she charged while we were pushing food over the fence. For the first time her hunger overrode her fear, and she wanted to shoo us away. And for the first time she was trumpeting for all her worth. But instead of a clear, clean call, she was honking like a strangled goose.

David and I looked at each other. Now we knew why she had been silent. In screaming for help, calling to her mother and aunts, the poor, lonely creature had destroyed her vocal cords. She really was a special case.

To try to lighten the mood, we affectionately named her ET, short for the French *enfant terrible* or "terrible child."

Even though she started to tolerate me a bit more, ET was still deeply unhappy. We could feel her fear and loneliness. It hung heavy around the entire *boma*.

Then it seemed as if our tiny progress had been no help to her whatsoever. She slid hopelessly back into despair. She began to walk endlessly in large figure eights, unaware of us or her surroundings. Her sadness bordered on a grief too deeply rooted to penetrate. She was so depressed I feared she might die of a broken heart.

45

I set out in the Land Rover to look for the herd. They were the only solution to ET's misery.

"Coooome, Nana, coooome, *babbas*!" I called out once I saw them about three hundred yards away. Nana looked up, her trunk reaching into the air. She figured out the direction my voice was coming from, and she and the herd started ambling through the bush toward me. As they advanced, I marveled at these magnificent, beautiful creatures—fat, gray, and glowing.

I needed their help, and I was going to try something I had never done before: get them to follow me.

As they approached, I eased the Landy ahead for about fifty yards. Nana stopped, perplexed about why I was moving away. Then I called them again and, after milling about for a bit, she came toward me. As she got near, I drove off again. Again she stopped, confused.

I called, "Coooome, Nana!" willing her forward. I told her it was important, that I needed her. Would she understand the urgency from my tone?

Amazingly she started to follow me. She eventually kept

coming, without me even calling out to her. The family followed fractionally behind. Through my rearview mirror, I saw nine elephants following me. I was the pachyderm Pied Piper. Deep in the African bush, I had a herd of wild elephants following me because I wanted and needed them to. It was all so unbelievable, yet it was happening. Oh, how I loved them.

The herd following the road.

Three miles later we were at the *boma*. The herd had stayed the course.

I stopped thirty yards from the fence, and Nana came toward me. She paused for a moment and then saw the youngster. Nana looked back at me, as if, perhaps, to acknowledge that she realized why I had called her. Then she walked over to the fence and let out a long set of rumbles.

ET stood as still as a tree, peering at the herd through the dense foliage. She lifted her trunk to get their scent for a few minutes. Then she ran excitedly to where Nana was standing at the fence. This was ET's first sighting of her own kind in a year.

Nana lifted her thick trunk over the electric fence, reaching out to ET, who responded by raising her own trunk. I watched, captivated, as Nana touched the troubled youngster. ET shyly acknowledged Nana's authority. By now the rest of the curious herd had come forward. Frankie also reached her trunk over the electric wire. And there they all stood, rumbling and grumbling in elephant talk.

This went on for twenty minutes. Scents and smells were exchanged, and introductions were made. What happened next left me in no doubt that ET's troubles were over.

Nana turned and moved off. She deliberately walked past the gate where she had originally pushed over the poles to get out. I had no doubt she was showing ET the exit and also telling me to open the gate.

But with all the elephants around we could not get anywhere near the gate. We could do no more than watch as ET moved along with them from inside the fence until she reached the far end and could go no farther. She backtracked up and down the fence, honking sadly, trying to find a way to join them. It was heartbreaking to watch.

Now we could get near the gate, but would ET allow us to open it? No chance. Every time we approached, she thundered across, enraged. It was as if we were preventing her from joining the others.

Eventually ET stopped. She was exhausted by her continuous stampedes. So we moved in quickly, removed the horizontal gate poles and electric strands, and then retreated once more.

Nana, who had been waiting and watching in thick cover nearby, came out of the bush around the other side of the *boma*, with her family following in single file. Deliberately and slowly she once again walked past the now-open gate. ET rushed out of the thicket but missed the exit. She followed them on the inside of the fence until she could go no farther again. Her despair was wrenching, but there was nothing we could do until she figured out that the gate was her sole exit point.

This time Nana didn't wait. She kept going toward the river, and just as I thought we would have to close the *boma* for the night, ET backtracked to the gate and was gone, her trunk twitching just inches off the ground as she chased after the herd's scent.

We switched off power to the *boma* fences and packed up. Half an hour later as we were driving home, we saw them moving away across the open savannah. They were still in single file, but already the pecking order had been established. ET was second to last, holding the tail of the elephant in front of her. Mnumzane was behind her. He was comforting her by resting his trunk on her back as they moved along.

46

I spent as much time as I could out in the bush near the herd to see how ET would settle in with her new family.

Unfortunately ET went ballistic whenever I came near, especially if I climbed out of the Land Rover. She just couldn't believe that her matriarch was permitting an "evil one" to get close. She quivered on full alert, ready to charge at a moment's notice. This meant that I had to be as low profile as possible. She may have been a youngster, but she still weighed a couple of tons and I wasn't sure what Nana's or Frankie's reaction would be if she decided to attack me. I was in uncharted territory. There was nothing to do except be patient and let ET's anger diffuse itself.

While ET may have been as mad as a snake at me, she was absolutely ecstatic with her new family. To see this previously depressed creature joyously bonding with the other youngsters, pushing, pulling, and playing with all the physicality that elephants so enjoy, was simply phenomenal.

Mnumzane, however, still got shooed off if he got too close to the rest of the herd. I reckoned I was his best friend by default. Whenever I drove past, he would trumpet and chase after me. I always stopped, and he would then block the road, trapping me for as long as possible as he grazed around the Land Rover. I loved our "chats" together, but they didn't rid him of his loneliness or unease. His newfound relationship with me was not natural and it concerned me a little.

It *was* natural, of course, for an elephant bull to be pushed out of the herd at puberty. Eventually he would get over the rejection and join a loose group of other bachelors. But we didn't have other bachelors, and to bring in a dominant bull to provide Mnumzane with a father figure was not something KZN Wildlife would consider. New rules set by KZN Wildlife demanded a larger reserve for elephant bulls. Mnumzane was stuck living partly on his own and partly on the fringes of the herd.

One day he was grazing a few yards away from the Landy when I got a radio call from the lodge. Penny, our bull terrier, was missing. With Max at my heels, I searched around the lodge. Penny normally responded to my whistle, but today there was only silence. I feared the worst.

I made my way down to the watering hole where, suddenly, I saw her tracks. I followed them down into the riverbed and then saw some way upstream. I shuddered and got goose bumps. I knew something was wrong.

Then I saw it. With its knobby, gray-green armor plating barely noticeable in the wind-rustled reeds, there lurked an absolute monster of a crocodile. A flash of white caught my eye. Just a few yards away, lying motionless in the water, was

Penny. My heart sank. It looked like she had been snatched and drowned by the croc.

There was no way I was going to leave my loyal dog there for the croc to eat. I edged closer. Crocodiles don't like loud noises, and they like being surprised even less. When I was barely fifteen yards away, I jumped up, screamed, and clapped my hands. With a *whoosh* of its huge tail, the croc disappeared underwater. I waited until it resurfaced some distance downriver. Then I waded in to retrieve Penny's body for a proper burial.

The next day I went back down to where I had found her. Penny was too smart to have let any croc stalk and grab her. I wanted to figure out what had really happened; I was determined to stay and study the clues until the mystery was solved.

I examined all of Penny's tracks. Her footprints clearly showed that the sand had been scuffed backward. She had been charging into the river. At first this didn't make sense, but then it came to me. The croc hadn't gone after Penny. Instead, my brave, insane, beautiful dog had attacked the crocodile. She had deliberately rushed into the water and taken on a killing machine twenty times her size. Bush signs do not lie.

I believe Penny saw a crocodile and recognized it as a threat to all of us. With the limitless courage of her breed, she willingly gave her life to protect all that was important to her, all that she loved. Penny went to her death doing what she considered was her duty.

She was one of the finest and bravest creatures I have known.

47

On a quiet day I took the opportunity to visit the herd. I was on foot, and by the time I saw ET, it was too late. She hurtled out of the bush like a missile, and there was no way I could scramble to the safety of my vehicle in time. I was in big trouble. I had no option but to ignore every screaming instinct in my body and force myself to hold my ground and face the charge. Despite my mounting panic, some small voice in my head kept reminding me that any attempt to flee would be a deadly mistake.

All of a sudden Nana, who was about twenty yards off, moved across at surprising speed for her bulk and blocked ET's charge with the broadside of her body. The youngster stumbled and was knocked off course. Clumsily she regained her balance, meekly swung around, and lumbered to the back of the herd. Nana resumed grazing as if nothing had happened.

I stared, barely breathing, pulling body, soul, and nerves back together. That was certainly a first for me. In fact I had never heard of it before: One wild elephant had blocked the charge of another elephant to protect a human. Over the past few weeks I had been wondering how to handle ET's constant aggression, and here was Nana, doing it for me. She was teaching the youngster not to hurt me.

Before ET's arrival, I had planned to start cutting back on my visits to the herd. My sole purpose had been to rehabilitate them in the bush so that they would remain truly wild elephants, supremely at peace in their environment. Wild elephants that become too accustomed to people can generally become unpredictable and, therefore, can be extremely dangerous at times. They will almost always end up getting shot. For this reason, I insisted that none of my staff ever interact with them, and I never interacted with them to entertain lodge guests.

Nana pays me a visit.

My original idea was that once the herd was settled, I would gradually withdraw until there was no more contact. I believed I had been almost there.

But ET was still a major problem. While the herd comfortably tolerated and ignored Land Rovers cruising past, ET was doing the exact opposite. She regularly made threatening moves and gestures toward the vehicles, which was alarming the tourists and upsetting the rangers. Wilderness bush walks, which had become a favorite with our visitors, were now too dangerous to continue.

This meant I needed to spend more time with ET. So instead of cutting back contact as planned, I was now forced to increase visits.

I started working with ET from my vehicle. I approached her slowly and watched for her reaction. She would always go after me, whether it was two or three aggressive steps or an angry, headlong run, with her ears flaring and her tail lifted. In the *boma* I had purposefully backed off whenever she had done this in order to boost her self-confidence. Now she had to learn to respect me, and then all vehicles and humans.

Through trial and error I had learned several techniques on how to approach an aggressive elephant. In ET's case, I decided she needed to be challenged directly. I needed to confront her head-on.

I approached her in the Land Rover, stopped in front of her, and waited with the engine idling. As she started to charge, I quickly jerked the Landy forward at her, just a yard or so, once or twice. This was, in effect, saying to an elephant, "I'm not messing about here. I'm ready to fight. So back off."

Doing this always broke ET's aggression. Then I would lean out of the window and say in a firm but comforting voice, "ET, if you don't mess with me, we can be friends." I was essentially demonstrating my position of seniority in the herd's hierarchy.

I swear Nana and Frankie knew exactly what I was doing. They didn't interfere, unless they knew I needed their help. And it turned out I did.

It happened again. I was on foot, and ET caught me by surprise. She came charging at me out of a thicket. I had thought she was with the herd in the thick bush ahead, but she was on her own on the flank.

This time it was Frankie who reacted. She sprinted up alongside the galloping youngster and placed her tusks on ET's rump. This forced ET to sprawl on the ground in a cloud of dust. Frankie stood over her until ET clambered up and sulked off to join the others. To see Frankie—once the very definition of aggression—protect me was little short of astonishing.

Then there was a third full-blooded charge. This one was broken by Nana in a way I had never seen before. I was about thirty yards away from the herd, just sitting and watching them, when ET started to stampede toward me. To do so, she had to run past Nana, who was grazing a little way ahead. Nana heard the youngster coming and tilted her head. As ET began to build up a head of steam, Nana lifted her trunk and held a pose, waiting. When ET was close enough, Nana reached out and touched her ever so gently right in the middle of her forehead with the tip of her trunk.

ET stopped dead, as if she had been whacked on the skull with a sledgehammer. Yet all Nana had done was caress her.

48

Despite the charging incidents, ET was making progress. Working with her day after day was making a difference.

It turned out, though, that my work was only effective when ET was with the herd. She knew she stood no chance against me with Nana and Frankie around. Once when I was out following the herd on foot along with two junior rangers, I had no idea that ET had broken away from the herd. She was waiting in the thicket to ambush me. Suddenly I heard that awful sound as the bush came alive with snapping branches. ET galloped into the clearing, dipping her head in the awesome way that elephants do when they start a charge. Her prize was finally within her grasp—and without Nana or Frankie to stop her.

I looked at the Land Rover behind me. It was definitely out of reach. I shouted at the two young rangers, "She's coming! Don't move! It's okay! Just don't move." If ET's charge was a bluff and they ran, that could make her change her charge to a deadly serious act.

"No! No!" I yelled at ET. "No!" I raised my arms above my head, screaming at her as she thundered on toward us.

At the last moment she broke off. She swung away at a lumbering gait, her trunk high.

Then my heart sank as I watched her turn a wide circle and come at us again. I shouted to the rangers to continue to stand their ground. But I was talking to myself. Having just witnessed their first-ever up-close-and-personal elephant charge, the two young rangers had decided that to stand still for another one was the most insane thing in the world. They had hurriedly climbed to the top of a giant fig tree nearby.

That left me to confront a charging ET alone. Encouraged after seeing the rangers bolt and scramble up the tree, she was now more determined than ever.

Everything switched into slow motion. The shrieking, mind-numbing fear left my body and was replaced by a bliss-ful calm. That happens to me every time a situation with ele-phants turns hairy. I screamed and screamed at ET until she was virtually on top of me. Then at the last moment she went swinging past. I can tell you that she very nearly didn't pull out of that bluff in time.

She kept running and joined the herd, who were ambling across to see what all the fuss was about. Personally I thought that Nana could have reacted a little quicker.

I looked up at the two tree-hugging rangers. "Jeez! That was unbelievable!" shouted one from the top of the tree, giving me a thumbs-up. "I can't believe you made it. I thought you were a goner. Well done."

Yeah, thanks.

The herd was getting closer. The still-agitated ET was with them, so I hurried over to the Land Rover and drove it under the giant fig. I deliberately called Nana and Frankie to me. I was going to teach these two rangers a bush lesson, all right. By fleeing, they had put all of our lives at risk.

I talked to the elephants for a little while, joking with Nana for not being there sooner and speaking sternly to ET for what had happened. Then I drove off. I left the rangers in the tree with the herd right beneath them.

About three hours later while I was relaxing on the front lawn, the rangers got back. I didn't have to say anything.

Nor did they. They had learned their lesson.

49

The morning after a torrential spring storm with strong winds, I went to survey the damage. We had lost about five hundred yards of fencing on the reserve's eastern boundary. And we had no idea where the elephants had gone.

We finally sighted the herd on the opposite side of the river from where Brendan was working on repairs to the fence. I told Ngwenya to find a high spot and keep an eye on them.

A short while later I got the call I had always dreaded.

"Mkhulu! Come in!" said Ngwenya. "The elephants are out. They are outside."

I grabbed my radio and answered, "Where? What's happened?"

"On the northern boundary. They're walking along the fence, but on the wrong side."

I jumped into the Land Rover and called Musa, the fence ranger. I instructed him to follow me on the quad bike and we sped off, skidding on the barely passable roads.

We arrived twenty minutes later and I saw Nana right away. But she and the others were *inside* the fence. What was Ngwenya talking about?

I was so relieved it took me a moment to realize that something was seriously wrong. Both Nana and Frankie were pacing back and forth. Every few seconds they stopped and stretched their trunks over the top electric wires to shake the fence poles. The poles were the only parts of the fence they could reach without shocking themselves.

I counted the herd as I always do. There was one missing, but which one? Mnumzane? No, he was there. So I counted again.

Then I saw a movement on the other side of the fence. There stood little Mandla, Nana's firstborn son, all alone. I found out later that a flooded stream had taken out a small piece of the fence but had left one electric strand still standing that was just high enough for Mandla to walk under. It was too low for the rest of the herd. Once out, Mandla panicked and couldn't get back in.

Getting Mandla back in required some thought. The nearest gate was miles away, but a gate would be of little use, anyway, because it was just as likely that Nana would go out as Mandla would come in.

I drove closer and called out to Nana to let her know I was there. She stared at me, hard. My mind raced, trying to find a solution. If we didn't get Mandla inside soon, the herd would break through the fence. Without question. An elephant mother will do whatever it takes to ensure the safety of her babies.

How could we get Mandla in without letting the herd out? I looked at the electric wires and an idea came to me. If we cut the fence and then also the middle and bottom electric wires, Mandla could get in. But by leaving the top electric wire intact, it would prevent the adults from going out. The question was, would the top electric wire alone be enough to keep Nana and Frankie in?

Nana shook the fence violently again. Suddenly I heard hunting dogs bark. There was a hunting party somewhere out beyond Mandla. Nana heard them too, and she stopped rattling the fence. Instead, she spread her ears to absorb every sound.

The hunters were on their own land and in themselves not a problem. What concerned me was that if the dogs got the scent of Mandla and started to harass him, Nana would tear through the fence like a bulldozer.

But there was a more immediate issue: how to open the fence and cut the electric wires near Mandla with a herd of agitated elephants breathing down our necks?

We moved fifty yards away from the elephants, cut a hole, folded back the fence, and cut the bottom two electric wires. But call her as I might, Nana refused to come to me and move away from Mandla.

Finally, after more than forty minutes of me calling, asking, begging, and pleading, Nana ambled over to me and the hole in the fence. Mandla followed his mother on the other side of the fence, found the hole, and scampered back into the reserve.

Every one of the elephants crowded around him, touching him with their trunks, fussing over him, and rumbling. It was heartwarming to watch the care and affection being showered on him after his ordeal.

50

One afternoon, Mnumzane was browsing at the side of the road, and I was about ten yards away, hanging around the Land Rover and saying whatever came into my mind, both of us content in each other's company. It was one of those days when you just felt like hanging out with a friend, enjoying the warmth of sunshine and companionship. As usual, I did all the talking, and Mnumzane did all the eating. Something had changed, however, and I couldn't quite put my finger on it.

I had come to see Mnumzane because that morning one of the rangers told of a huge ruckus among the herd, complete with trumpeting and screaming that could be heard a mile away. I had just checked on the herd, who were grazing a few miles off, and they seemed fine. Mnumzane seemed calm, too. But there was something else. His insecurity, which at one time you could almost feel because it was so intense, seemed to have vanished. He seemed to have a newfound sense of self-assurance.

Mnumzane walked over to me until he was about ten feet away. There was no doubt he seemed more confident. And with him towering almost five feet above me, I needed every ounce of warmth and reassurance he dished out when we were together.

Mnumzane lifted his trunk toward me. This was extremely unusual for him. He seldom put out his trunk, and if he did, he didn't like me to touch it. He then turned and moved off into the savannah. That too was different. I had always been the first one to leave our bush sessions, and Mnumzane often tried to block my way by standing in front of the Land Rover.

That evening, the elephants visited the watering hole at the lodge. The chance to watch these lords of the wilderness up close was always such a treat for the guests. During this particular visit, I saw exactly why Mnumzane was now so self-assured.

The rest of the herd was already drinking and splashing around when Mnumzane emerged from the bush. With his head held high, he moved swiftly toward the watering hole. That was strange, I thought. He usually skulked around the edges.

Nana looked up and saw him. To my intense surprise she moved off, rumbling deeply to call the rest of the herd away.

But it was too late. Mnumzane picked up speed and smashed into Frankie—the herd's prizefighter—so hard that the blow thundered across the bush. Frankie was knocked backward and almost fell over.

Seeing what had happened to their champion, the other elephants started to hurry off. I caught my breath as Mnumzane swung to face Nana, his ears spread wide, his head held high.

Nana quickly placed herself between the threat and her

precious family. Then she turned and started reversing toward Mnumzane. She was not only sending a sign of submissiveness to him, but she was also bracing herself to best absorb the impact of his coming charge. I winced as she took the colossal force of Mnumzane's attack on her flank. Just watching took my breath away.

Satisfied that he now had the respect he believed he deserved, Mnumzane eased over to the water and drank alone. This was his right as the new alpha elephant. From now on he would always drink first.

Mnumzane had come of age.

Things changed on the reserve after that. Mnumzane no longer gave way to vehicles—or anything else for that matter. He would stand in the middle of the road and finish whatever he was doing before moving off in his own sweet time. Any attempt to move him along would result in a warning from him, which everyone always heeded. Nobody wanted to be charged by the big bull of the reserve. Everybody quickly learned bull elephant etiquette: stay away from him, or else.

Despite all that, to me, he was still the same old Mnumzane. Our bush meetings continued, but they were less frequent. He didn't trumpet to me anymore. And I was a lot more careful when I was with him. If I got out of the Land Rover, I would try to make sure that at least the hood of the car was between us. That didn't always work; sometimes he still wanted to stand next to me.

I loved this magnificent creature and was so pleased to see his insecurities and fears gone. He had had a tough time growing up without a mother or any father figure. At last, he had a role.

"You are a mamba," I said to him. "You are surely now a *real* Mnumzane—a real boss." He stood there motionless as I flattered him, gazing at me with those big brown eyes, as if accepting the compliment.

51

Mnumzane may have been the dominant bull, but Nana was still the boss of the herd. Not long after her clash with Mnumzane, Nana was involved in another one, this one with Thula Thula's other matriarch—Françoise.

I dashed out of the house to find Françoise at one end of her herb and vegetable garden, shouting at Nana, who was at the other end. Not only did Françoise love her garden, she also used what she grew there in the gourmet meals she cooked for lodge guests. Nana had broken into the garden through a weak link in the fence and—along with Mandla and Mvula— was gobbling up everything in sight.

Sensing, perhaps because I couldn't stop grinning, that I would be of no use whatsoever, Françoise rushed inside the house. She came out with some pots and pans and started to bang them together.

Nana looked up, startled at the clanging. She shook her head and stamped her drum-size front foot. She glared at Françoise, who glared right back. Nana simply continued to eat.

Realizing that her banging wasn't having any effect, Françoise got the garden hose. From a safe distance behind a fence she opened the nozzle and started to spray water at Nana like a firefighter. Nana, again, shook her head and stamped her foot.

Nana quickly got used to the high-pressure fountain and tried to catch the spray. That was it for Françoise. She heatedly told me and all the nearby rangers, who also could barely conceal their laughter, exactly how useless we were. Then she stormed back into the house.

I picked up the hose, relaxed the water pressure, and gently offered it to Nana. She came across and let me fill her trunk. Then she went back and totally wiped out the garden.

The next morning Françoise had an electrician over to fortify the fence. From then on the garden was off limits to anything with a trunk.

Françoise and the fence.

52

David led the way down an old game path and into a clearing. He showed me the body of a female rhino who, it appeared, had died recently.

I walked up to the immense, motionless animal, looking for a poacher's bullet wounds. There were none. And the rhino's horns were still intact. That surprised me, for I had expected them to have been sawed off, since poachers kill rhinos to get their horns.

I then checked the corpse for signs of disease or other causes of death. Except for some nasty, fresh gashes on her armor-plated hide, she seemed to have been strong and healthy.

Then I looked at the surrounding area. I was shocked. A tornado could not have done more damage. Bushes were crushed. Trees were sprawled and splintered everywhere. The ground had been ripped up. Nothing made sense. No rhino could cause such destruction. What had happened?

I instinctively looked to the ground for answers. Rhino spoor was everywhere, heavy in its tread, yet unnatural in its twisting and turning patterns. Then signs of an elephant jumped out at me—big, heavy pachyderm tracks, the aggressive, earth-wrenching footprints of an enraged bull in full cry.

Mnumzane!

I hoped against hope I was wrong. But the tracks told the story clearly.

To my left, a slight flicker in the bush caught my eye. A camouflaged rhino calf was silently watching from a nearby thicket. It was Heidi, the dead animal's two-year-old daughter. A rhino will fight to the death under most circumstances, but if she has a youngster, that's an absolute given.

"What a mess up!" I fumed, my words echoing harshly through the bush. "What did he do that for? The idiot!"

"We . . . we're not going to shoot him, are we?" asked David.

Shoot Mnumzane? No words could have shocked me more.

I knew, though, that was exactly what would happen in most South African reserves. Aggressive young male elephants, reared without the wise supervision of adult bulls, have been known to kill rhinos for no apparent reason. And when they do, they essentially sentence themselves to death.

Rhinos in South Africa are rare and very expensive. Elephants, on the other hand, are more plentiful and comparatively cheap. Because there is documented proof that an elephant who has killed a rhino before will do so again, most reserve owners will shoot an elephant, or set up a hunt for it, after its first kill.

Through one senseless, violent act, Mnumzane had made

himself an outcast, an untouchable. I couldn't keep him now. But I also couldn't give him away for love or money.

"No," I said, trying to convince myself. "We're not going to shoot him." We went over everything slowly. Heidi would be fine. She was big enough to survive without a mother and would herd with the other rhinos.

David and I both stood and took a long hard look at the hulking gray carcass and then left to go in different directions. He was going to gather the team to dehorn the once-magnificent creature. This would stop potential poachers from trying to get the horn once the word about the rhino's death got out. I was going to have a serious chat with Mnumzane.

As we left, I saw the calf trot out of the thicket and stand by her dead mother. Mnumzane had really messed things up big time.

It was another hour and a half before I found him browsing near the Gwala Gwala dam. I approached him slowly, pulled up about thirty-five yards away, got out, and leaned on the Land Rover's hood. I didn't call him, but he knew full well I was there. He chose to ignore me and to continue grazing, which is exactly what I wanted. I scanned his body with my binoculars and saw battle scars.

He had been gored in the chest, judging by the congealed blood I saw there. And there were deep grazes and scrapes on both his flanks. This had not been a brief encounter. The battle had been fierce and long, probably because he was not used to fighting. A veteran brawler of his size would have ended it with one thundering charge.

There also must have been plenty of opportunities for the rhino to escape, but because she had her calf with her, that wasn't an option.

Eventually Mnumzane finished eating and looked at me.

"Mnumzane!" I called out sharply. "Have you any idea of what you have done?"

I had never used that furious tone with him before. I needed him to understand I was extremely angry.

"This is a big problem, for you, for me, and for everyone. What got into you?"

Mnumzane stood motionless as I scolded him. It was only after I drove off that I saw him move away.

From then on I tracked him daily, staying near him as much as possible. If he approached, I deliberately drove off. I could see that bugged him.

Then through extremely good fortune, I found him near the scene of the crime. I immediately drove to the rotting remains of the rhino and, making sure I was upwind of the intolerable smell and in a good getaway position, I gently called him.

Obviously pleased to hear my usual friendly tone of voice again, Mnumzane ambled over toward me. I let him keep coming until he was right at the kill. Then I leaned out the window and lambasted him in a firm and steady voice. I stopped only when he, uncharacteristically, turned and walked off in the opposite direction.

There are those who will say that all of this was nonsense, that of course elephants don't understand, that I was wasting my time. But I believe Mnumzane got the message. He never killed or even hassled another rhino. Our relationship returned to normal, with Mnumzane showing up for our bush chats and even making an occasional appearance at the house.

© C. LOURENZ

Me and Mnumzane having a bush chat.

53

Nana's oldest daughter, Nandi, now twenty-two, was dignified, confident, and alert. She seemed to have inherited the qualities of a matriarch from her mother. She was also pregnant, and Mnumzane was the father. We were all excited and expected a big, healthy baby.

When Johnny, a new ranger, radioed me that Nandi had given birth, he sounded concerned. "We've just found Nandi down near the river but we can't see the baby properly," he said. "The herd's gathered around and won't let us anywhere near her."

I hurried down and saw the herd gathered in an unusually tightly knit and obviously flustered group.

I walked off into the bush, keeping my distance, trying to find a spot where I could get a peek through the group. When I finally got a glimpse of the brand-new baby, I saw that it was on the ground.

The fact that it was lying down set off alarm bells in my head. The infant should already be on its feet.

I needed to find out what was going on, so I started to approach slowly, carefully watching to see how close they would let me come. I was about twenty yards away when Frankie caught sight of me. She rose to her full height and took two or three menacing steps forward until she recognized me and dropped her ears. But she held her position. I could tell she didn't want me any closer. Once she was sure I understood, she turned back to the baby.

From where I had stopped, I could see what was going on. My heart sank. The little one was desperately attempting to stand up. Time and time again it tried, patiently lifted by the trunks of its mother, its grandmother, Nana, and its aunt, Frankie. But each time it rose halfway up, it fell back. Then it would try over and over again. This had obviously been going on for a while. My heart went out to the baby and the desperate family.

It was terribly hot, and with absolute rotten luck, the baby was lying in the middle of the only open space among the trees, right out in the blazing sun. To make matters worse, it was also on the hot sand instead of the grass.

There was nothing to do but wait, watch, and hope. I sent the rangers off on other duties, got myself a bottle of water from the Land Rover, and found a shady spot as close as I could to the elephants. I called out so they all knew I was with them.

I took out my binoculars and managed to focus in on the baby. It was a girl and the problem was clear. Her front feet were deformed. They had apparently folded over themselves in the womb, and each time she tried to stand, she was doing so on her "ankles."

After an hour, the little one was exhausted, and her attempts to stand were becoming weaker and less frequent. This did not deter her mom and aunt, who, if anything, renewed their efforts with each failure. By worming their trunks under the little body, they lifted the baby up and held her on her feet for minutes at a time. Each time they gently let her down, she crumpled to the ground again.

Elephants always find deep shade on hot days and stay there. Their humungous bodies generate a lot of heat, so keeping cool is a priority. I looked up at the sun and cursed. These poor animals were in its direct blast. Yet none moved off for the shade of trees that were barely twenty yards away. Even the younger elephants, who were doing little more than watching, stood in the midday solar furnace, guarding the baby. And no one left for a drink of cool water at the river, which was less than half a mile away. Everyone's sail-like ears flapped overtime, fanning as much air as possible in an attempt to cool off their overheated bodies.

Then I noticed that the baby was permanently in the shade of its mother's and aunt's shadows. Not just because they happened to be standing around her, but because they were taking conscious care to do so. They were slowly shifting their positions to ensure the struggling infant was always out of the direct heat. While the sun arced through the sky, I watched, amazed, as they all took turns acting as an umbrella.

Three hours later, the baby started to give up. She didn't want to be moved anymore and trumpeted pitifully each time family trunks lifted her. She was tired beyond measure.

After a while, Nana stopped, and they all just stood there, with the baby lying motionless in front of them. Through my binoculars I could see she was still breathing but had fallen fast asleep.

Wildlife can deal with hardships that would destroy a human without a blink. This little elephant had gone through the trauma of birth, spent half a day in a blazing new alien environment, and hadn't even had her first drink. Yet she was still alive, still fighting.

But she must have been nearing the end. Somehow I had to get her away from the herd. They were doing the best they could, but this little creature needed sophisticated medical care. With the best will in the world, Nandi and Nana could not fix the baby's feet. Her only chance was with us, and even that was uncertain.

But how could we get her away from the herd? An elephant's maternal instinct is extremely powerful. We could not remove a baby from its mother simply by driving up and snatching it.

So what could we do? Short of opening fire and trying to scare them off with bullets, which would destroy my relationship with them forever, there was no other way. Perhaps if it was just Nandi . . . but certainly not with Nana and Frankie around.

In the late afternoon, when the day had cooled just a bit, the elephants started again worming their trunks underneath the baby, trying to lift her onto her feet. They kept it up until nightfall, agonizingly failing each time.

I drove the Land Rover in closer and beamed the head-lights onto the scene to help them, watching in awe. They never gave up. They had been trying for nearly twelve hours now. Their persistence was absolutely phenomenal.

Toward midnight, the baby was pitifully weakened. I resigned myself to the fact that there was nothing I could do. She was not going to make it. I called out a good-bye, saying I would return, then drove back to the house and went to bed, expecting the worst when I woke the next morning.

54

The next day, I returned as dawn broke. Incredibly the herd was still there, still trying to get the now-almost-completely limp body to stand. The dedication of these magnificent creatures was beyond comprehension. My respect for them and what they were doing was infinite.

The sun started to climb, and by ten a.m. I knew we were in for another scorcher. Still, they continued. But what more could they do?

A few minutes later, Nana backed off a few paces for the first time. She stood alone, as if taking stock of the situation. She then turned and walked off without stopping. Her trunk dragged, her shoulders stooped. She was the picture of defeat. A decision had been made. Nana knew they had done all they could. She knew it was over. Despite their best efforts, the baby was unable to stand. Thus, it couldn't survive.

The rest of the herd followed Nana. They were soon out of sight, on their way to the river. They had been on wilderness ER for more than twenty-four hours without food, drink, or rest. Few humans could do that.

Nandi stayed behind. As the mother, she would be there

to the end, protecting her baby from hyenas or other predators. She made sure her crippled daughter was in her shadow and stood still, her head down, exhausted and resigned to her firstborn's fate. She was determined to protect her infant to its last breath.

Through the binoculars, I saw the baby's head move, just barely. My heart pounded with excitement. She was still alive! With the herd gone, a crazy plan came into my head.

I sped to the house, loaded a large open container on the back of the Landy, and filled it with water. Then I threw a bag of fresh alfalfa in the back and had Brendan summon the rangers.

"Okay, guys," I said. "This is what's going to happen. I'm going to reverse right up to Nandi, give her a sniff of the water and alfalfa, and then slowly move off to try to draw her away from the baby. She hasn't had a drink or anything to eat for twenty-four hours, and she's been baking in the sun. She's starving and thirsty, so she may just follow me. There's a sharp corner in the road about thirty yards off, and if she follows me there, she won't be able to see the baby. That's when I want you guys to sneak the truck in from the other side as fast as possible, load up the baby, and speed off."

I paused for a moment, scanning their eager faces. "If Nandi sees you taking her baby, there won't be enough of you left for me to bury. So if you're not comfortable with this, don't come with me. It's very dangerous. I really mean that."

There wasn't a moment's hesitation. "We're in" was the unanimous reply.

I nodded my thanks. "Okay. I've phoned the vet and he's on his way. I have also put a mattress in the back of the truck for the baby."

We quickly drove to the spot, got into position, and went over every aspect of the plan once again. "We've only got one chance," I reminded them. "Reverse in so you can drive out going forward if she sees you. We need one driver and two men in the back to load the baby."

I, at least, had some protection. Nandi knew me, and I was carrying food and water. For the rangers, it was a different story. Nandi didn't know them. On top of that, they were stealing her baby.

55

I got in the Land Rover and began to drive in reverse toward Nandi. When I got closer, I called out to let her know it was me. Her first reaction was uncharacteristic. She moved between the baby and the approaching Landy and then charged, trumpeting loudly to scare me away, kicking up a cloud of dust as she came toward me. She had never come at me before, so I stopped, leaned out of the window, and started talking to her soothingly. As she walked back to her baby, I gently started reversing toward her again. She reacted with another noisy stampede. I kept talking to her, and the third time I reversed, her charge had no steam at all. As she turned away, I saw her physically react as she caught the irresistible scent of fresh water and food. She stopped and looked at me.

"Come, *baba*," I called gently. "Come, beautiful girl, come on. You're hot; you haven't had anything to eat or drink for more than twenty-four hours. Come to me."

She paused and then took a few tentative steps forward, ears straight out, hesitantly checking everything. Then she walked up to the Landy, dipped her trunk into the trough, and sucked in a trunkful of water, which she squirted messily into her mouth, spilling it everywhere in her haste. She drank without stopping, and I moved forward very, very slowly. Without hesitation she followed, slugging down gallons of water as we moved along. She was so thirsty, she still hadn't stopped when I managed to lead her around the corner, out of sight of her baby.

"Go, go, go!" I whispered into the radio. "I can't see you, so neither can she. Let me know as soon as you've done it."

I kept talking to Nandi, calming and distracting her with my voice. Then, for what it was worth, I told her what we were doing. "Unless I take your baby, she's going to die. You know that and I know that. So when you get back she won't be there, but if we save her, I will bring her back to you. That I promise."

I have no idea whether she understood me, but tone and intention can communicate far more than mere words. At least I knew I felt better that I told her what we were doing.

A few minutes later, I got a call. They had gotten the baby into the truck.

"Great! Well done," I said. "Get her up to the house. I'm going to stay with Nandi for a while."

Nandi drank every drop of water and then tucked into the alfalfa. When she finished, she looked at me in acknowledgment and walked back to where she had left the baby. I followed her and watched as she started to nose the ground. With her superb sense of smell, she must have immediately caught the scent of the rangers. She sniffed around for a few long minutes, stopped for a while, and then she turned and slowly moved off in the direction of the herd.

I know that if she had smelled hyena or jackal there was no way she would have reacted so calmly or left the scene so quickly. She would have followed the scent with a vengeance, never letting up.

My hands were shaking. I couldn't believe we had done it. Thanks to my fearless rangers, we had taken a baby elephant from her mother.

Now all we had to do was save her life.

56

When I arrived back at the house, the baby was lying motionless in the shade on the grass. The vet was inserting a drip with fluids into a vein behind the baby's ear.

"She's barely alive and very dehydrated," he said. "The next few hours will tell if she makes it."

I made a few phone calls to find out what milk substitute a wild, orphaned baby elephant would take. We got the recipe from Daphne Sheldrick's famous animal orphanage in Kenya, and I sent a ranger into town to buy the ingredients as well as some jumbo-size bottles.

While I did that, Françoise started to turn the spare bedroom, right next to ours, into an elephant nursery. She scattered straw on the floor to make a firm mattress for the baby to sleep on.

I went back to the baby, who Françoise had decided should be named "Thula," and inspected her front feet. They were crumpled in on themselves.

"She's huge," said the vet. "In fact, too big. That's why her feet were squashed back. She was simply too big for the womb, and her feet had nowhere to grow. But the bones aren't broken, and the muscles are intact and loose enough to manipulate into the correct position. Hopefully they'll straighten out with some exercise."

He walked around her. "Her ears are also worrying me a touch. They've been burned raw by the sun and sand, and she may lose the fringes. I'll prescribe some ointment."

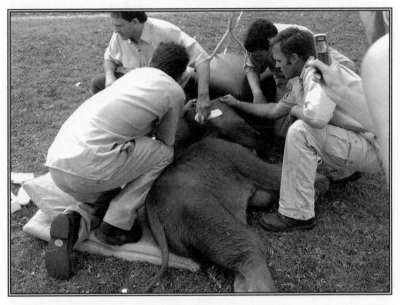

Baby Thula being put on a drip shortly after her rescue.

Just then, Thula lifted her head quite strongly. A drip with fluids is a wonderful thing with wildlife. Sometimes it works so powerfully it's like watching an animal spring back from the dead, and so it was with Thula.

Holding the drip, we carried her to her new room. She instantly fell asleep on the mattress.

Johnny, one of the rangers, stayed with her around the

clock until she was healed. Orphaned elephant babies need constant companionship. Without it they rapidly decline, both physically and emotionally. Johnny, who had joined us only a few months back, was going to be her temporary mother.

The next morning Thula took her first giant-size bottle from Johnny. She drank the whole thing.

The following day she was much stronger, so Johnny made a canvas sling and hung it from the towering marula tree on the lawn. We gently carried Thula outside, then slipped the sling under her stomach while she protested. We lifted her up with our improvised pulley, and Johnny eased her deformed limbs forward. We then lowered her with her feet in the correct position.

We had to strengthen her front feet or else she would die. So there she stood, wobbling at first, but gradually gaining some balance. We repeated this procedure several times between meals. By evening she was standing steadily with the aid of the sling.

I whistled softly. Perhaps we could save her after all. Perhaps I would be able to keep my promise to the herd. The progress this tough little infant had made in just one day was inspirational.

The next morning, Thula started taking uncertain steps, supported by the sling. By the third day, she was walking on her own, though she moved slowly and fell down a lot. Yet Thula never complained. She always seemed cheerful, almost laughing in an elephantine way as she struggled to get up. Her courage was absolute. Her cheerfulness amid what we can only assume was constant pain was simply unbelievable.

Within a week, although limping badly, this brave little creature was hobbling around the lawn with our gardener, Biyela, following behind her with a large golf umbrella to protect her from the sun. She had captured Biyela's heart. From now on it seemed his mission in life would be to keep the sun off her.

As the days went by, Thula got stronger and was soon regularly taking the bottle, even though feeding times sometimes redefined the word *chaos* in our house. Johnny would back Thula into a wall, put his arm around her neck, and ram the bottle into her mouth, squirting the vitamin-enriched milk into her system while she fought him every inch of the way with all of her 270 pounds. Johnny often landed flat on his back with milk spraying all over the place, while Thula bolted for the door to seek consolation from her new best friend, Biyela.

But the fact that she took the bottle regularly was a huge plus. It is often difficult to get an orphaned baby elephant to do that. I think she did so because she was essentially a happy creature, and we had also created a caring environment around her. Françoise, in particular, lavished constant attention on her, and Thula adored her in return. She followed Françoise around the house like a giant, love-struck puppy.

The only problem was that Thula broke everything she could reach. We soon learned that anything not nailed down would be trashed. If she didn't pull it onto the floor with her trunk, she bumped it down with her bulk.

As Thula got stronger, her limp lessened. Apart from having some trouble lying down, Thula was healing beautifully. Now her biggest problem in life was trying to figure out what that strange appendage waving in front of her face was all about. An elephant's trunk pulses with about fifty thousand muscles. Thula was endlessly fascinated by her trunk. She flapped it about as a human baby would with a doll.

Although I had instructed everyone that she should never be alone, I could have saved my breath. Johnny was always there, and off-duty staff members regularly came to the house to make a fuss over her. Everyone loved her spirit, and Thula thrived under the utter devotion of her new family. Despite what had to be constant pain as her feet slowly straightened out, she always seemed to be smiling. Even Max—who would fight any creature for no reason other than that it was there—followed her around the lawn on her daily walks, happily wagging his tail.

Late one afternoon, when I was walking her through the bush outside the garden, getting her used to the longer grasses, thorns, and trees that would be her future home, I saw the herd appear at the top of the road. They had decided to come to the house for one of their visits.

The timing could not have been worse. I was well outside the electric wire, and to be caught with Thula in the open by her mother could be disastrous. If I made a run for it and abandoned Thula, they would no doubt whisk her off. If that happened, she would die. Her feet were still ill-equipped for life in the bush. It would be a death sentence for her, even if Nandi lagged behind with her.

The only thing going for me was that the herd didn't know Thula was alive. They had come for a social visit, not to find their baby. I had to move fast.

I urged Thula to go to the nearest gate in the electric fencing as quickly as possible. Luckily I was downwind, and the herd didn't scent us while Thula stumbled along behind. If the wind had been blowing the other way, it could have provoked a stampede from the herd.

We managed to make it to the gate, and I passed Thula on to Biyela. Then I turned to watch the approaching herd.

When they arrived, Nana's trunk shot up like a periscope, the tip twitching until she fixated on where Thula had just ambled out of sight. She turned and rumbled. Nandi and

Me with Baby Thula outside the room she lived in following her rescue.

Frankie joined her and smelled the air Thula had left behind. They were like detectives at a crime scene.

I went to Thula's room and made sure she was closed in with Johnny. Then I called a ranger to double-check that the fence's current was on. I then waited, hoping they would leave.

Twenty minutes later they were still there, and I felt I could no longer ignore them. If I let them see Thula, it might prompt something we could not handle. When elephants believe their babies are in danger, they're uncontrollable. So what could I do to satisfy them but still keep Thula with me until she was fit and strong enough to be returned to them?

I didn't know. But I felt that, at least, I should let them know that their baby was alive.

I went to Thula's room, took off my shirt, and swabbed it along her body. Then I put it back on and wiped my hands and arms all over her.

I walked back down to the fence and called the herd. Nana came over first. As her trunk swept just above the electric wire in greeting, I stretched my hand out as I usually do. Her response was remarkable. The tip of her trunk paused at my hand, and for an instant, she went rigid. Then her trunk twitched as she sucked in every particle of scent. I offered her both hands and she snuffled them and every inch of my shirt. Nandi and Frankie stood on either side of Nana, their trunks snaking around as they too picked up the scent that let them know that Thula was alive and close by.

All the while I talked to them. I told them how we had

helped Thula cheat death. I told them what was wrong with Thula's feet and why she had to stay with me for a little while longer. I told them we all loved her because she was so courageous and happy. I told them that they could be proud of their newest little member, who was fighting so bravely for her life. I told them too that, for some completely random reason, even Max had befriended her.

We had come a long way together, this herd and I, and talking to them had been a crucial part of that process. And why not? Who am I to judge what elephants understand? Besides, I personally find this communication most satisfying. They evidently like it too, responding as they do with deep rumblings.

Now they listened and read whatever they could from my shirt. Then these three magnificent elephants stood before me like a jury weighing evidence.

After much thought, they moved off, and I could tell they were relaxed and unconcerned. I'm not saying this lightly. I have seen unhappy elephants. When the ladies left, I knew that they were happy. I knew that they could have stormed the fence, electric or not, if they had felt otherwise. I could feel a warm glow ignite inside me. They trusted me. I knew I could not let them down.

57

The weeks passed. Thula was doing well, reveling in the affection and care heaped on her by Françoise, Johnny, and Biyela. Inside the house, she was Françoise's shadow, particularly in the kitchen where she would dip her trunk into anything Françoise was cooking. She still broke everything. The rangers' weekly shopping trip to town now included lugging back mountains of crockery to replace all those damaged by Thula. But what could you do? How could you get angry with a brave creature that never gave up? That never complained?

Outside, Biyela was her hero. With his multicolored golf umbrella constantly covering her, the two became inseparable. In fact, Biyela would sulk if Thula remained in the house for too long.

Thula was our mascot. She had an energy and vitality that tapped into the philosophy of the reserve: Life was for living.

Then one morning Johnny called from Thula's room, where I found her struggling to get up.

"She can't stand," he said, pushing and pulling her to try to get her on her feet. I hurried to help him. Eventually, after much squealing and protesting on Thula's part, we had her up. She tottered briefly, then limped outside.

Biyela and his umbrella appeared as if by magic. As we followed him and Thula, I saw that it took far longer for her limbs to loosen up. Biyela saw this too, and I watched as he spoke softly into her weakly flapping ears. I then realized she wasn't just stiff in her feet. She was in severe pain, and it wasn't the same pain she had bravely fought before. Now her right hip also seemed to be troubling her. This was serious. I called the vet.

"Short of doing X-rays, which is impossible, I can't tell you what's wrong," he said. "Nothing is broken, but she has badly inflamed joints in her front feet and hip, probably caused by the way she walks."

He then prescribed some medication and instructed us to ease off on long walks.

The next morning and the morning after that, it was the same. Thula couldn't stand up. A week later she wouldn't drink. Johnny—unshaven, wild haired, despondent, and soaked in the milk he was trying to coax her to take—summed it up: "She's just not interested anymore."

I looked at Thula, who was in the corner facing the wall, listlessly swinging her little trunk back and forth. She was also suffering from thrush, which is an extremely uncomfortable yeast infection in a baby's mouth. Thula hated the nasty-tasting ointment we spread over her tongue and gums each day.

By this time, Johnny was exhausted. So I took the bottle from him and tried to ease it into Thula's mouth, but with no success. Then Françoise, whom Thula truly loved, tried. She was gentle with her, but Thula still wouldn't take the bottle.

As Johnny said, she wasn't interested. Once a feisty little fighter, she suddenly seemed to have given up. I had no idea why, except that perhaps the pain she had put up with in her courageous quest to live was now simply unbearable.

The next day, Thula took a quarter of a bottle of milk, just a fraction of what she needed, but her taking even a small amount gave me hope. I prayed her strong spirit would return.

That evening the vet came out and put Thula on a drip. Two days later, despite more drips and encouragement from the entire staff, Thula sank into bottomless indifference.

Early the next morning, an inconsolable Johnny told us that Thula had passed away during the night while he was with her.

Thula's death affected everyone, especially Françoise. I have never seen her sob so bitterly. We've had lots of animals live with us over the years and we have been close to them all, but with Thula something was different. The elephant's cheerful ways and her refusal to surrender until the end had inspired everyone. She had shown us how life could be joyous, despite pain. How it could be meaningful even if it was short. Thula had shown us how life should be lived for the moment.

Thula left behind a storm of sorrow that would not let up for many days. Johnny took her body out to the grasslands to allow nature to take its course.

I went out later in the Land Rover by myself to find the

herd. When I did, I led them to the carcass. They gathered around. This time I didn't speak. I didn't have to tell them what had happened. For a moment I held my head in my hands. I had let them down. When I looked up, Nana was outside the vehicle's window. Her trunk was raised in her familiar greeting pose. Nandi was next to her. We looked at each other. Then they moved off.

Thula's remains are still there. Every now and again Nana leads her family past, and they stop. They sniff and push the bones around with their trunks in an elephant remembrance ritual.

58

Max was now fourteen years old and too old to accompany me into the bush he loved so much. The old warrior, who had survived poachers, snakes, and feral pigs double his size, had painful, chronic arthritis in his hind legs. He could barely walk.

I had been told by Françoise and a few close friends that I had to face up to the fact that Max was no longer bulletproof. He was very old and not going to last much longer, but it was just too awful for me to consider. I got him the best veterinary help I could, but recently he had all but stopped eating. Sadly I knew his time was coming.

Even so, I was surprised to see Leotti the vet's car parked in the driveway one day. She and Françoise were sitting next to Max's basket in the lounge. Françoise seemed on the verge of tears.

Max tried to get up to greet me, but he fell over. He tried again. . . . He wouldn't give up.

Leotti, who had treated Max throughout the years, looked at me and shook her head.

"Françoise phoned me about this. Lawrence, I know you love him but it would be cruel for this to carry on."

She stood up. "I will be waiting outside."

As she closed the door, Françoise put her arms around me and squeezed for a moment. Then she too left.

I sat down next to my beautiful boy and lifted his rugged spade-shaped head onto my knee. He looked up and licked my hand the way he always did. Even now, Max was still a superb dog.

Max, my Staffordshire bull terrier, when he was young.

He and I sat for about ten minutes, just us together. I told him how much I loved him, how much I had learned from his courage and loyalty, and that the life in him was eternal. He knew exactly what was happening; we were too close for him not to. I braced myself and called out to Leotti.

She came in. The syringe was ready, and she administered the injection as I held Max.

I was inconsolable.

59

A month or so later, a young ranger on a game drive with two guests unexpectedly ran into Mnumzane coming in the opposite direction.

Mnumzane started to amble over toward the vehicle. The ranger panicked, reversed too fast, and smashed into a tree. They were stuck with Mnumzane coming straight at them. To the frightened ranger's credit, he didn't reach for his rifle. Instead he told his passengers to sit tight and not make a sound as Mnumzane strode up to the vehicle. I know firsthand that this is one of the most frightening sights imaginable. Mnumzane lightly bumped the Land Rover, and his tusk actually grazed one of the guest's arms. Somehow the man didn't scream.

Showing great presence of mind, the ranger jumped off his seat in the front of the vehicle and sneaked around to the other side to help the guests get out. Then they all fled into the bush. Mnumzane fiddled around the Land Rover for a bit without causing any damage and then moved off. Once they were sure he was gone, the three crept out of their hiding places and hurried back to the lodge.

From all accounts, Mnumzane was just acting curious and not aggressive, so I didn't take it too seriously. After that encounter, however, Mnumzane occasionally started to approach our open game-drive vehicles for guests. I heard that he was never angry and that the rangers would simply drive away as soon as he approached.

The bigger problem was that this was totally out of character for Mnumzane. He simply was not behaving as an elephant. Elephants automatically ignore humans as long as we don't move into their space.

Then I discovered the reason for Mnumzane's sudden interest in game-drive vehicles. It turned out that, without my knowledge, two of our young rangers had seen me with Mnumzane. I had deliberately kept my interactions with him private, or so I had thought. These rangers thought they would try to get up close to him, too. So they began teasing him. They played "chicken" with him, daring one another to see who could drive closer to him before speeding away when he approached. It never occurred to them that they were teaching him a dangerous, bad habit. He now considered the shouting and revving of engines as a direct challenge. As a result, the tourists' game drives were forced to move off whenever they saw him.

The most non-negotiable rule on the reserve was that no one was allowed to have any self-initiated contact with the elephants. Anyone who disobeyed that rule would be instantly dismissed. Both rangers had resigned before I found out what they had been doing. I hope they have since embarked on careers far removed from wildlife.

A little later, a trainee lodge manager left without notice. The dust had barely settled as he sped from the reserve when I heard that he too had been using a game-drive Land Rover to approach Mnumzane, trying to imitate my call. Mnumzane had always been a very special case, and continuous teasing by strangers was dangerously altering his attitude to humans. My concern mounted.

I had recently gotten a brand-new, white Land Rover station wagon and decided to take it for a test drive. It performed beautifully off-road, but getting around a grove of trees forced me to make an extremely tight 360-degree turn. I had just about completed this when suddenly I felt unaccountably apprehensive.

An instant later, Mnumzane towered next to me. He had appeared silently from the shadows—as only an elephant can—and was simply standing there. I looked up into his eyes, and my heart skipped a beat. His pupils were as cold as stones. I quickly called his name repeatedly in greeting. It took ten chilling seconds before he started to relax. I completed the turn, talking continuously to him as he gradually settled down and let me go.

I drove off with a heavy heart. Things were not the same anymore. Perhaps his behavior had been because he had not recognized the new vehicle. I hoped so. But he shouldn't be approaching any of our vehicles, let alone acting aggressively toward them.

Then in another incident, our lodge manager, Mabona, was driving up to the house when Mnumzane appeared from nowhere and blocked her path. Doing exactly as she had been trained, she cut the engine and sat motionless. Mnumzane moved to the back and leaned on the car, shattering the rear window. The crackling glass surprised him and he backed off. This gave Mabona enough time to turn the key and accelerate away.

After this, we hacked out a dozen or so outlets on the road to the lodge where vehicles could rapidly reverse and turn around if necessary. I also had all encroaching bush on the track cleared so we could see Mnumzane before he got too close.

This worked. Mnumzane now had no contact whatsoever with any human except me. Everything started to return to normal, but I was still worried. I began spending more time with him, trying to reassure him and get him to settle down. With me, he was always the same friendly accommodating giant that I loved. He seemed okay.

However, my senior rangers remained unhappy. They wouldn't go near him, and all walking safaris were stopped if Mnumzane was anywhere in the area.

A few weeks later a journalist and good friend asked to film me interacting with Mnumzane. I agreed only on the conditions that the camera crew's vehicle be out of Mnumzane's sight and that no one spoke during the entire episode.

When we found Mnumzane, I drove forward and got out of my new Land Rover, leaving a young ranger in the back of the vehicle. I called out, and Mnumzane started to amble over. I had some slices of bread in my pocket to throw to the side when I wanted to leave. I had recently taken to doing this with Mnumzane. Although I dearly loved him, when on foot, I would turn my back on him only if he was distracted.

As he approached, I studied him and decided he was fine. We had a wonderful ten minutes or so interacting, chatting about life. Well, I chatted while Mnumzane contentedly browsed. When I decided to leave, I put my hand in my pocket for the bread. But it had hooked in the material of my trousers, and I looked down trying to yank the slices out.

At that moment it was me, not Mnumzane, who was distracted. He suddenly moved right up against me, and I got the fright of my life. For not only was he almost on top of me, his entire mood had changed. Something behind me had disturbed him, possibly the young ranger in the Landy, and he wanted to get at him. There was meanness in the air.

I quickly threw the bread on the ground. Thankfully he moved over to snuffle it up, and I retreated.

By the time I got back to the film crew, my heart was pounding like a drum. I knew his temper was on a razor's edge. Something had changed with him.

I would soon realize how much.

60

A few weeks later, I was taking some visitors on a game drive in my new Landy. We spotted Heidi, the rhino who had been orphaned as a calf, slinking into the bush. We were crawling slowly along when, out of the twilight, the herd appeared and crossed the road fifty yards ahead.

"Elephants," I said, switching on the spotlights.

It was the first time my two passengers had seen an elephant, let alone a herd. I switched off the engine to let them savor the moment.

Then came Mnumzane, bringing up the rear. I saw that he was now in musth, ready to mate. When a bull elephant is in musth, his hormone levels skyrocket and his behavior can become dangerously unpredictable. This is especially true if the bull is following females, just as Mnumzane was doing.

Nana was leading her family toward Croc Pools. I waited for about five minutes to make sure they were well off the road before I started the Land Rover and moved forward.

Suddenly, the man in the passenger seat started shouting, "Elephant! Elephant!"

I strained my eyes searching the headlight-lit road in front of me. I didn't see anything.

"Elephant!" he shouted again. He pointed to his side window.

There was Mnumzane, barely three yards away in the dark. Prompted by the shouting, he stepped forward and lowered his massive head right onto the window as if to see what all the noise was about. With instant dread, I saw his eyes. They were stone cold.

Mnumzane then prodded the window with his trunk, testing it. Realizing that at any second he was going to shatter the window and crush my passenger, I slammed the vehicle into reverse while desperately pleading with the hysterical passengers to calm down. When the vehicle reversed, the glass skidded across Mnumzane's tusk. Then with a jarring bang, his tusk got snagged by the edge of the door. Mnumzane lifted his head and trumpeted in rage. I knew we were now in grave danger.

As far as Mnumzane was concerned, the car had "attacked" him. In retaliation, he swung in front of us and hammered the front protection bar so hard that my head smacked the windshield as I shot forward like a crash-test dummy. Then he put his huge head on the bar and violently bulldozed us back twenty yards into the bush. He stopped only when the rear wheels jammed against a fallen tree.

I opened my window and screamed at him, but it was pointless. I watched in horror as he backed off sideways to give himself space to build up speed, then I lost sight of him as he moved out of the headlights. At least the guests had stopped yelling. All three of us were silent.

There was only one way out. As Mnumzane set himself up for the charge, I revved the engine until it was screaming and tried to wrench the Landy out of his way. Too late. He came at us in an enraged charge. The shock of the impact shook my teeth as he smashed his tusks into the side of the Landy just behind the back door and heaved us up and over.

Ka-bang! The Landy smashed down on its side, then flipped over onto its roof and into a thicket as Mnumzane drove on with his relentless attack. Another colossal charge flipped us back onto our side.

My shoulder was lying on the grass through the broken side window, and the guest in the passenger seat was practically on top of me. I tried to gather my senses. I wasn't injured, but my biggest concern was that this wasn't over. Bull elephants have a terrifying reputation for finishing what they start. As if to confirm this, just inches away, Mnumzane stomped around the upturned vehicle in a rage.

I had to snap him out of his red mist of anger. Amid all the confusion, I somehow remembered that elephants that have been exposed to gunfire sometimes freeze when they hear shots. I also knew that it could go the other way, that the gunfire could prompt a final lethal attack, but I had no choice.

Twisting around, I drew Françoise's tiny pistol from my pocket just as the Landy shuddered from another blow. I pointed at the sky through the broken windshield and fired . . .

again and again and again. My last-ditch plan was that, if he got to us, I would shoot the final slugs into his foot and hope that the pain would divert his attention long enough for us to somehow get out and run for our lives.

To my eternal relief, he froze. It had worked. As he hesitated, I called out to him, but I was trembling so much my voice was way off-key. I gulped lungful after lungful of oxygen until I was steadier. Then I tried to speak again. When my voice was calmer, Mnumzane recognized it, and his ears dropped. The anger visibly melted from his body.

I then told him that it was okay, it was me, and he had frightened me, and he didn't need to be angry anymore. He slowly came right up to where I lay on my side in the Landy. His feet, practically the size of trash-can lids, were inches from my head. All he had to do was lift his foot and that would be it. I aimed my puny gun at his foot and then watched, captivated, as he pulled out shards of glass from the shattered windshield and then gently reached in and put his trunk onto my shoulder and head, touching me, smelling me all over. All the while I talked to him, telling him we were in terrible danger, and that he must be careful.

He could not have been more gentle. After a while, he walked off and started browsing on a nearby tree as if nothing had happened.

I reached for the radio only to find that it had been smashed off its hinges. In the darkness I found it and fumblingly reconnected the wires and got it going. I whispered a Code Red. I described where we were and what had happened. Then

I turned the volume down. I didn't want any loud noises to unsettle Mnumzane.

Luckily there were rangers on a nighttime safari close by who had heard the shots. They were with us in minutes. But whenever they approached, Mnumzane started to challenge their vehicle, keeping them away.

Knowing they carried a rifle, I whispered strict instructions into the radio that, despite how bad everything looked, under absolutely no circumstances was Mnumzane to be shot. They must wait until he left.

But he wouldn't leave. He kept approaching the Landy. Each time he did, one of the guests would panic and frantically climb over to the opposite side of the vehicle. This just prompted Mnumzane's interest even more. He would walk around and bump the vehicle, which would make the poor guest scramble back the other way. It was horrifying to lie there absolutely helpless in the dark with this giant stomping around outside, hitting the vehicle. Every now and then I would call out to him, and he would come around to my side and stand quietly for a while. Then he would go back, worry the guests, and continue to chase off the rangers who were trying to come to our aid.

I started to despair, but then I heard a ranger anxiously calling out on the radio, "The herd is here; the whole herd is here. They're coming straight toward you. They're going to your Landy. What must we do? Over."

"Nothing," I replied. "Just wait."

This was good news, not bad news as the ranger thought.

Leaning forward out of the vehicle, I could just see Nana and Frankie, followed by the herd. I repeatedly called out to them.

Unusually, they ignored me. Without breaking stride, they walked right past us and then, to my astonishment, they surrounded Mnumzane, jostling him away from us. He could easily have butted them off—he certainly had the strength—but, amazingly, he didn't. From my cramped horizontal position on the ground, I could hear them rumbling. I have no idea what the communications were about, but moments later Mnumzane left with them.

When the herd was about fifty yards away, the rangers sped up, climbed on top of the Land Rover, and pulled us out via the smashed side windows, one by one. Thankfully—and incredibly—no one was hurt.

As we drove off, I watched the elephants walking with Mnumzane, the undisputed dominant bull, submissively in tow. Given that adult bulls are loners, it was most unusual to see him with them. I have no doubt that Nana understood what had happened and that she and Frankie intervened to get him away. Not only for our good but for his. She probably saved our lives.

As we passed by, some forty yards away, Mnumzane lifted his head sharply and took a few angry steps toward us. That he again showed aggression toward the Land Rover concerned me infinitely more than my wrecked vehicle. I had a big problem on my hands.

61

Our traumatic escape had me going in a dozen different directions trying to figure out what to do. Predictably some wildlife experts said that Mnumzane should be put down immediately, that he was an accident waiting to happen. They claimed if I didn't do it now, someone was going to get killed.

Once again, I rose to Mnumzane's defense and said that all he had done was come to my vehicle as he had done hundreds of times before. He then became confused by strange voices shouting and, because he was in musth, lost it when the Landy suddenly reversed and hit his tusk. My proof was that as soon as he had heard my voice, he had stopped his craziness and had come over to see if I was okay.

I refused to shoot him. Instead, I started to put measures in place to ensure his and everyone else's safety. We cleared out every inch of bush and shrubbery for thirty yards on each side of all roads between the house and the lodge. Now, if he was anywhere near the road, he could be seen from a long way off. At night, I had a ranger with a spotlight drive well ahead of any staff vehicle to check if he was around.

But there was no need. Mnumzane had gone deep into the bush alone and stayed there, almost as if to atone for his outburst.

The herd, on the other hand, were just being wild elephants, doing things that contented elephants do, such as pull down whole trees for grazing, wallow in mud baths, and provide great game viewing. Even ET had settled down, and I took comfort from this success. After a few weeks of no trouble, I dared to start thinking that Mnumzane had learned something from the incident and could be saved.

Then early one morning, I was radioed by a safari-drive ranger who told me that his vehicle had broken down, and he had left it in the bush while he went to get parts. When he returned, the vehicle was off the road. It had been smashed and overturned.

Even before I got there, I knew what had happened. Mnumzane's spoor was all over the place. He had found the vehicle and destroyed it. Despondent, I surveyed the damage.

A safari Land Rover has no roof, which makes it easier to see game. If an open, roofless vehicle had been turned over, people inside could have been killed. Mnumzane attacked an empty Landy. There was no reason to think he wouldn't attack one with passengers in it.

I tried very hard to justify what he had done. But there was no way out. It was over, and I knew it.

I took a slow, lonely drive home and called a friend to borrow his rifle, numbed by the words that came out of my mouth. After I hung up, I was appalled at my decision, but I knew in my heart that we had reached the end of the road. If I left it any longer, someone was going to die.

I didn't want to make any mistakes. So I drove into town and collected the rifle along with eight rounds of ammunition. Without telling anyone, I went out onto an adjacent property, marked a tree, and fired three practice shots. An hour later, I found my big boy grazing peacefully near the river.

At the sound of my car, he looked up and came ambling over, pleased to see me as always. Feeling absolutely treacherous, I got out, readied the rifle on the open door, and took aim. His familiar features looked completely out of place in the telescopic sight. When he got close enough, I just stood there—wracked by emotion, tears flowing freely—unable to pull the trigger.

I couldn't do it. I stuffed the rifle in the car as he stood by, warmly radiating greetings in that special way he had. I gathered myself and said good-bye to him for the last time. I told him we would see each other again one day. A few moments later I drove off, leaving him standing there, obviously bewildered by my hasty departure.

The next morning, two sharpshooter friends I had phoned arrived. They were retired professional hunters who were conservationists. They knew exactly what they were doing.

"You're not coming with us?" one asked. "You sure you don't want to do this yourself?"

"I tried. I know him too well." My voice was dead. "He's now completely lost the plot," I said, not wanting to go into the details.

An hour later, I was standing outside on the lawn looking over the reserve I love so much when I heard two distant shots. As the finality of it came crashing home, I was seized by a terrible loneliness, both for my beautiful boy and for myself. After nine years of friendship, I had failed. He had gone to join his mother, whose violent death just before he came to Thula Thula he never really recovered from.

I forced myself to go to where Mnumzane's immense body was lying. I was pleased he hadn't fallen badly, but was lying on his side as if asleep.

"It was painless. He was dead before he hit the ground," said one of the shooters. "But we had a bit of a fright at the last moment as he suddenly came at us, and it was touch and go. There's something wrong with that elephant. You made the right decision."

I looked at the magnificent body. The ground and sky still pulsed with his presence.

"Good-bye, great one," I said and got back into the Landy and went to call the herd, to bring them, to let them see what I had done.

What I had had to do.

62

"These things always seem to happen in threes," I thought mournfully a couple of days later. I was thinking about the deaths of baby Thula, Max, and Mnumzane in the space of little over a year. I was comforted by my belief that although they were gone physically, they would always be part of this piece of Africa. Their bones would always be in this soil.

With the exception of elephants and crocodiles, which can live for seventy years, animals generally do not live long. Lions live only about fifteen years, as do impala, nyala, and kudu. Zebra and wildebeest can reach twenty, and giraffe a little more. Many smaller animals live very short lives. Some insects live for just weeks or even days.

Each spring, the bush comes alive with new life. Thula Thula becomes a giant nursery. Thousands of caring mothers of all shapes and sizes bring a new generation into the world. And they need to because, despite its beauty, the wilderness is a hostile environment. Only the fittest, wisest, and luckiest will reach old age. Death is a part of life. This is reality, and I like it that way. It's natural, uncluttered by material things, and it helps me to maintain a wholesome perspective on my own existence and that of my friends and family.

I was sitting on a termite mound near a grove of acacias, still deep in thought, when a Land Rover approached and Vusi, now a senior ranger, got out. He told me he had just driven past Mnumzane's body.

He paused for a moment, looking at me directly. "There was only one tusk."

"What do you mean only one!" I asked. "Where's the other?"

"It's gone. Stolen."

"How did that happen?" I was shocked to the core.

"It was there yesterday evening. I saw it myself, and today it's gone." He continued staring at me, a rare gesture for rural Zulus, whose culture demands that eyes be averted. I think he was as shocked as I was.

"We searched for hundreds of yards around the body. Then I had every inch of the fence checked, and there are no holes cut by poachers. Nobody broke in last night."

I stared back, astounded.

"Also, I advised security, and every car today has been searched. I didn't want to tell you until I was sure."

"That's unbelievable," I said, thinking back to our early poaching days.

"It's still on the reserve," replied Vusi confidently. "One of the staff must have it and has hidden it somewhere here. Someone with a vehicle. I saw the lights near the body last night, but it was gone before I got halfway there."

Just then Ngwenya walked up carrying the remaining tusk over his shoulder. He lowered it heavily onto the ground.

"There is something that will interest you," said Vusi, abandoning the topic of the theft. "Feel here," he said, and he knelt down next to the magnificent piece of ivory, his fingers running lightly over its length. "There is a bad crack."

I crouched next to him. I had always known that the tip of Mnumzane's tusk had a slight crack, but since this is fairly common with elephants, I didn't worry much about it.

But then I followed the path of Vusi's fingers with my own and whistled. On closer inspection, the crack was much bigger and deeper than I had realized. In fact, the tusk was splayed right open at the end, and the blackened interior was visible. A tusk is just an extended tooth. And just as with a human, a break like that in a living tooth is a magnet for infection and absolute torture.

"*Yebo*, Mkhulu," said Vusi. "There was a big swelling right at the top of the tusk, deep inside. I cut it open. It was rotten."

I whistled again, for now everything made perfect sense. Poor Mnumzane had been in so much pain for so long that he just couldn't stand it anymore. That's why he became so evil-tempered. And I suddenly realized, that's exactly why he went berserk and flipped the Land Rover over. When I reversed, I jarred his excruciatingly sensitive tusk on the edge of the Landy's window. He must have seen blinding stars in his agony. It took the gunshots from my pistol just to yank him out of it.

I sat down on the lawn and put my head in my hands. Although unusual to do with a wild elephant, all it would have taken was a dart of sedative, a good vet, and some antibiotics, and we could probably have taken his pain away. And he would have still been with us. A picture of him contentedly browsing before me during our "chats" flashed through my mind. He basically had been a happy creature—despite the tragedies he had witnessed in his short life.

I shook myself out of it, forced myself to focus, and then stood up.

There was nothing I could do about it now.

"Let's get the tusk cleaned and then store it in a safe place," I said to Vusi. "Now, at last, we know what happened to him and why he went crazy."

"*Yebo*, Mkhulu."

"And let's find that other tusk!"

I walked away astonished that one of my own staff could even think of stealing Mnumzane's tusk at a time like this. I had wanted them mounted as a pair in the lodge as a commemoration of his life.

We never found the tusk. But that doesn't mean I'm not still looking.

63

I was finally making progress with my years-long discussions with the *amakhosi* and their people about joining their lands together with Thula Thula and Umfolozi to create one large game reserve. This was an idea I had first thought of back when I purchased Thula Thula.

At that time, when I looked at a map of the area, I had been struck by how much unused land there was that came right up to the borders of Umfolozi and Thula Thula. The land belonged to six different Zulu clans, and I had been meeting with and talking to each individual clan for many years. I hoped to convince them that not only would a large reserve be wonderful for wildlife, but it would also create many much-needed jobs for their people.

I knew this was an ambitious undertaking, but I had no doubt it was the right thing to do. I just needed to be patient and persistent. And now, it looked like my approach was paying off.

One afternoon I received a surprise phone call from *Nkosi* Nkanyiso Biyela. *Nkosi* Biyela was the key to my plan's success. He was, by far, the most powerful *Nkosi*, or chief, in the area, and the Biyelas controlled the biggest chunk of the land.

He wanted to meet at Thula Thula the following day to talk about the game-reserve project. I eagerly accepted.

When he arrived, we drove through the reserve, observing the lush wilderness and robust wildlife.

"Whose land is that?" asked the *Nkosi*, pointing to a stretch of heavy bush just outside our boundary.

"It is yours."

"Good! Then I would like to join it with you," he said. As simple as that.

He went on to say that he would also join the land to the north with Thula Thula. "We will then do the joint project you have spoken of for the benefit of my people," he said. Again, as simple as that.

"Thank you, *Nkosi*."

He offered to help me secure the tract of bush and thorn on my western boundary. In just a few minutes—completely out of the blue—he had described most of the land that made up my dream African game reserve.

There was one last piece of the puzzle, the most important piece. It was Mlosheni, an eight-thousand-acre section of land that ran right up to the White Umfolozi River, the gateway to Umfolozi. Once we had that, we could lower the fences between Umfolozi and Thula Thula and have one massive reserve.

"Mlosheni," I said.

"What of Mlosheni?" he asked.

"Mlosheni will join us to the Umfolozi reserve. It is important."

"Of course! I have spoken with my *izinduna*; it is already agreed," he said matter-of-factly. "The animals will migrate as they used to before the fences were put up."

We shook hands. I was elated, scarcely able to believe what I was hearing. This project would do more for his people and for wildlife than anything that had ever happened before. My mind raced, thinking about the benefits to everyone. *Nkosi* Biyela would lead a coalition of traditional communities in this new plan.

I knew too that, while this agreement represented a fundamental breakthrough that had been years in the making, there was still a lot of work to be done. Many lengthy meetings lay ahead. But at long last, he was fully committed. Now it would happen. *Nkosi* Biyela's word was, without question, what we needed most.

That evening in the lodge we continued discussing what we were calling the Royal Zulu project and what it could do to regenerate our area. I felt that Mnumzane's soaring spirit would be part of a magnificent new reserve that would be Africa as it should be: wild, beautiful, with people and animals living in harmony. To me, the new reserve would be a monument not only to Mnumzane, but also to Max and baby Thula. They had all shown the qualities most needed in the fight for our last remaining wild lands: courage, loyalty, and, above all, perseverance.

It was an evening I will always remember. A vision of what Africa can be, coming to life. Royal Zulu would at last become a reality and, I hoped, a cornerstone of conservation in Africa.

AFTERWORD

◆✗◇✗◇✗◇✗◇✗◇✗◇✗◆

They say you get out of life what you put into it. But that is only true if you can understand what it is you are getting. One day, as Nana's and Frankie's trunks snaked out to me over the fence, I fully understood that they have given me so much more than I have given them. I saved their lives, but what I have received from them in return is immeasurable.

From Nana, the glorious matriarch, I learned how much family means. I learned how wise leadership, selfless discipline, and tough, unconditional love is the core of the family unit. I learned how important one's own flesh and blood actually is when the cards are stacked against you.

From Frankie, the feisty aunt, I learned that there is nothing more important than loyalty to one's group. In the blink of an eye, Frankie would lay down her life for her herd. The love and respect she receives from them in return for her courage is absolute.

From Nandi, I learned about dignity and how much a real mother cares. She was prepared to stand over her deformed baby for days without food or water. She kept trying to help her, refusing to surrender.

From Mandla, I saw how tough it can be for a baby to grow up on the run in a hostile world and how his devoted mother and aunts had ensured that he made it. He has now reached puberty and is about to be kicked out of the herd, as nature decrees. He is about to face new challenges.

From Marula and Mabula, Frankie's children, I saw firsthand the results of good parenting despite adverse circumstances. These beautiful, well-behaved children are what we, in human terms, call "good citizens," something that is often in short supply in our world. They see how their mother and aunt treat me, and in return, they give me the respect one would give to a distinguished relative. I love them for that.

From ET, I learned forgiveness. I had managed to reach out to her through her heartbreak and distrust, but only because she let me. Somewhere along the way she recovered her life and, in the process, taught me how to forgive, as she had forgiven humans for the horrors they had inflicted on her own family before she came to us. When she became a mother, she proudly showed off her baby. I made a special fuss over her.

And, of course, there had been Mnumzane, my big boy, who had become one of my dearest friends. Like anyone, I have things I regret in life. To me the biggest regret I have is that I did not somehow guess that an excruciating tooth infection had been the cause of him going "rogue." I console myself knowing that no other game ranger would likely have worked that one out, either. Indeed, he would have been shot out of hand a lot earlier on most other reserves.

But perhaps the most important lesson I have learned is that there are no walls between humans and elephants except those we put up ourselves. And that until we allow not only elephants, but all living creatures their place in the sun, we can never be whole ourselves.

POSTSCRIPT

Lawrence Anthony, elephant whisperer (1950–2012).

The day after Lawrence died in March 2012, the elephants, led by Nana, arrived at his house. They had not done so for some time as Lawrence had deliberately withdrawn. He wanted them to be truly wild. Yet they came, in an eerie vigil, which to think of still gives me goose bumps.

As Lawrence's son Dylan said, "They had not visited the

house for four months; it must have taken them hours to make the journey. They all hung around for about two days before making their way back into the bush."

Some people may say that the animals were merely wandering past. But we know better—don't we?

Today the elephants are thriving. The herd is now thirty members strong, an astonishing feat when you consider that the first seven animals arrived at the reserve in 1999 with a suspended death sentence.

Six months after Lawrence passed, another calf was born. The rangers called her Andile, which means "they increase" in Zulu and is as true a description of Lawrence's legacy as you will ever get.

After Andile arrived, an amazing thing happened. As soon as she could stand, the herd started moving toward the house where Lawrence had lived. When they reached the river, however, it was flooding. The herd stopped and milled on the banks. Rangers watched, wondering what had happened. The giants could easily wade across the brown swirling waters, but something was preventing them.

Then, for the first time, the rangers saw the baby, and it became clear. The herd couldn't enter the swollen river because Andile was too tiny and would have drowned. The animals were agitated and wanted to cross. It was a straight route to the main house—but they dared not proceed.

The rangers understood. Nana and the herd had set off to introduce the new arrival to Lawrence, which had been a ritual when he was alive. Even though the elephants knew

Lawrence was no longer around, as shown by their silent vigil on the day after his death, the ritual remains with every new baby born.

Some people may say that's a coincidence; the animals were simply going to the river to drink. But we know better—don't we?

There is also a new bull on the reserve, who was brought in to take on the role of patriarch after Mnumzane died. His name is Gobisa, and he has filled beautifully the void left by Mnumzane. Nana's son Mandla and Gobisa hang out together, the pachyderm equivalent of dudes at the wilderness shopping mall. As Lawrence had hoped, Gobisa has taught the young male manners. They do not try to be macho juveniles, turning over Land Rovers, throwing their weight around just as some teenagers without strong father figures sometimes do. They are now content in their enormous power. So much so that Mandla is now the alpha male on the reserve.

The spearhead of Lawrence's legacy falls upon his wife, Françoise, and the team of dedicated rangers, guards, and employees of Thula Thula. They are the keepers of the flame. It is what they do every day of their lives.

One aspect of Lawrence's legacy is that he irrevocably changed people's perceptions of our fellow creatures on this planet outside the perimeters of conservation. When he spoke at gatherings, whether attended by celebrities or the village book club, the message was the same. For people who said "I can't," Lawrence had a simple answer: "You can." Get involved. Join conservation movements that actually do something rather than relying on media gimmickry; lobby your local government official; plant a tree.

Or most important, just go outside and look. Breathe. Through Lawrence, legions of people today now know that the wilderness is not somewhere out there. It's in your soul.

That is what Lawrence's legacy is all about.

—Graham Spence

ACKNOWLEDGMENTS

To Mom for a lifetime of encouragement; Jason, Dylan, and Tanny for their care; and for my wonderful grandsons, Ethan and Brogan; Gavin; Mandy, "the Chosen One"; Jackie; and Laurie and Wilkie from Cambodia. Terrie, Paul, and Cameron. Graham for his insight and skill. The Malby family. Hilary and Grant. Jonno and Stan for fun friendships and refusing to agree on anything ever. *Nkosi* Nkanyiso Biyela for his wisdom; Ben and the Ngubane family for their wonderful friendship; *Nkosi* Phiwayinkosi Chakide Biyela for his foresight and leadership. Barbara, Yvette, and all the Earth Org staff for taking up the challenge. Ian Raper for his leadership. Mehdy and the Zarrabeni family; Dave Cooper, the game rangers' game ranger. Bella. Elmien. Marion Garaï. The Bruwer boys. Mabona, Vusi, Ngwenya, Bheki, Bonisiwe, Biyela, Zelda, Brigitte, and all the incredible Thula Thula staff. David and Brendan for being there and doing it; and to Peter Joseph, Ingrid Connell, and Lisa Hagan for their confidence and support.

—Lawrence Anthony